Also available by Carol Leyland

The Charlotte and Me Series

Charlotte and Me

Deceptive Hearts

Deceptive Hearts

All rights reserved. No part of this book may be used or reproduced in any form whatsoever without written permission except in the case of brief quotations in critical articles or reviews.

This book is a work of fiction. Names, characters, businesses, organizations, places, events and incidents either are the product of the author's imagination or are used fictitiously. Any resemblance to actual persons, living or dead, events, or locales is entirely coincidental.

Printed in the United Kingdom.

For more information contact :

carolleyland73@gmail.com

Book design by Josie Hammond Stones

Cover art by Carol Leyland

ISBN 978-1-0-6856072-9

First Edition: October 2024

Dedication

This book is dedicated to the children lost to time, without names, their memories gone. I hope this in some small way gives a voice back to the voiceless.

Trigger warning

This book deals with issues around alcoholism and mental health.

Chapters

Chapter One – Field of Dreams 1
Chapter Two – To dance by candlelight 14
Chapter Three – Heart breaker 23
Chapter Four – Moving on Up 34
Chapter Five – The Wildness of the Moors 40
Chapter Six – In the footsteps of the Bronte's 52
Chapter Seven – The Shibden Hall Pilgrimage 60
Chapter Eight – Dancing at Tod Disco 67
Chapter Nine – Pinging all the way home 83
Chapter Ten – Crisis in Stonegate 90
Chapter Eleven – Unpacked and Picked 103
Chapter Twelve - Redressing the Balance 115
Chapter Thirteen – Hope and all its friends 125
Chapter Fourteen – What Dreams are Made Of 131
Chapter Fifteen – The Signing 145
Chapter Sixteen - Reopenings 168
Chapter Seventeen - Plans Ahoy 180
Chapter Eighteen – Two Soups 188
Chapter Nineteen – To control and deceive 205
Chapter Twenty – The Thrills but no Spills 211
Chapter Twenty-One – Waiting for the axe to fall 223
Chapter Twenty-Two – A race against time 232
Chapter Twenty-Three – At Last There's Peace 236
Chapter Twenty-Four – It ain't over til it's over 243

Acknowledgements

Forever grateful to all my friends and family who have supported me this last year whilst writing this book. Writers and musicians are not wrong when they say the second book or album are the hardest. I have spent more time worrying about this one than I thought I would, but here it is all finished and ready for you to read.

Many thanks go out to my friends Krista, Christa, Lou and Mel, Mandy, Clare, Katie, Suzanne, Jo and Jill for listening to me and sending support along the way. To Sue for proofreading and avoiding the rude bits.

Special thanks to Josie and Heather for their help with the front cover.

To Maggie, for lovely writing retreats and hollibobs to help with the process by the seaside.

To my children Damian, Rowan and Eleanor, thank you for not reading the first book to spare our blushes but your support has been so special to me.

Also to Mariah Counts an amazing American singer for permission to use her song 'Everything I Need' within the book. A song that means a great deal to me and the words always bring a tear to my eye. Do check her out.

To the readers of Charlotte and Me who gave me such brilliant feedback and telling me how much you loved it and the women in it. They became my friends along the way so I hope you all enjoy their continued journeys.

And finally to my fiancée Claire. Thank you for the love, care and encouragement to get the book finished and for proof reading at the end.

Chapter Twenty-Five – Was it really I love you?................ 265
Chapter Twenty-Six – To build the future 282
Chapter Twenty-Seven– When the end has a beginning .. 290
Epilogue... 300

Chapter One – Field of Dreams

Standing at the 5-bar gate Alice inhaled nature in all its glory. On the drive to the campsite they'd passed farmers toiling in the fields bringing in that year's harvest and leading the corn to their barns. It was the part of her life that Alice missed the most, being immersed in the daily changing of seasons, and how life evolved and kept going regardless of the weather. She let out a big sigh.

The past year had been a whirlwind of emotions. Romantically the past twelve months had been long and happy, she and Charlie had grown even closer, their love had deepened, and they very rarely spent nights apart.

However, in the past couple of months Alice had been feeling more tired and breathless. Last year she'd been diagnosed with a faulty heart valve, and now more symptoms had appeared and she was seeing the heart specialist more often.

But the weekend plans were not about that, it was for fun, well-earned R&R and a chance to spend quality time with good friends.

The trip to a small women's festival had been Holly's idea. Now they wouldn't exactly be camping, as women over the age of 50 they preferred the comforts in life, so they'd all opted to hire ready erected bell tents which came with access to private showers and loos not that far away.

Personally Alice hadn't been camping since she was five years old, when the accommodation was a tent with plastic roll down windows, which took up a massive pitch because it was the size of a small bungalow. Inside there were fabric zip up doors that separated two bedrooms from the living area. It was like taking a house on holiday, with fold up chairs, tables and a mini kitchen inside the bedrooms they each had a camp bed with huge sleeping bags as her mother had been paranoid about creepy crawlies.

Her dad on the other hand had loved camping. He had been a whizz with the portable gas stove, and he always cooked up a storm. Years later the battery light they always took away with them had come in very handy during the 1970s strikes, where they would be put to good use whilst they played Monopoly, or monotony as her dad called it.

The camping phase didn't last long, like most of her mums fads and obsessions. Her mum was very much like Hyacinth Bucket (a UK television character in a series called Keeping Up Appearances) and she behaved as though she was posher than she actually was. So once the tent was sold, whenever they went away on holidays, they'd stay in the up-market chalets instead. So here she was decades later doing it all again, hopefully without the wasp infestation and the Portaloo hell.

Alice opened the gate to let in the two cars: one containing Charlie in her Jeep and the other her two best friends Jen and Holly in their Ford Focus. Closing the gate behind them Alice jumped back into the passenger seat and put her hand on Charlie's thigh, which she knew was her favourite driving position. She was so sexy when she was driving, one hand on the wheel using just the heel to steer. It was one of the very many things she loved about her.

They drove slowly over the grass field towards where the tents were situated and the organiser with her clip board stood directing traffic and giving out instructions. Seeing them approach she came over to the driver's door telling them where to park and checking them off her list, pointing out which bell tent was designated for them. Each tent was a different pastel colour, sat like a row of shabby chic flags dotted across the landscape. Bunting adorned every one, and in front was a large fire pit with logs surrounding it to chatter into the night.

After parking the car they all walked back to their respective tents, Alice and Charlie's was peach coloured and Jen and Holly's was pale yellow three tents apart.

'Aw we aren't next to each other sis,' said Charlie.

'Glad we aren't. Don't want to be kept awake by you two do we Holls?'

Holly smiled. 'I couldn't possibly comment.'

'Tactful as ever,' said Jen opening up the flap of their tent, and with a bow swept her arm in an act of service towards the entrance. 'You're tent awaits Holls.'

As they disappeared into the depths of the tent, Alice linked arms with Charlie and they went to investigate theirs. It felt like a Tardis inside, with a huge a bed in the centre with nightstands and battery lamps, a large hessian mat filled the floorspace with multicoloured rugs strewn around. Alice's eyes lit up when she saw the wood stove where a black kettle sat on top. Two small armchairs and a large squishy bean bag finished off the furniture, leaving a lot of space to wander around. She doubted either of them would make any use of the beanbag, not without a hoist as back up to wrench them out of it.

'Oh my god it's so sweet, isn't it lovely!' she exclaimed.

'It's ace, love it, great idea of Holly's to come. We can pretend to be hippies!' said Charlie.

Alice giggled. The idea of Charlie being a hippy was beyond imagination.

'You could try love,' she said smiling.

'Tune in, turn on, burn out and all that.'

'Definitely can do the burn out part,' said Alice. Her world had been exceedingly busy. The launch of her biographical history book about Charlotte and Hester who had lived in her house a century prior had been very well received. So much so she'd done a flurry of interviews both for archaeological and historical magazines, and had been lined up for book signings and talks. On top of that her job as a lecturer had been really full on, so it was no surprise that she was feeling really tired. This break away was just what she needed.

'Right you, go put your feet up and rest a bit, let me go and get the bags and set things up, that alright love?'

'Sure that you don't want a hand?'

'Nah, me and Jen will sort it. Get your feet up!'

'Yes boss,' smiled Alice. She liked it when she got a bit forceful. Her nickname for Charlie had been Tigger from the beginning, she was always bouncing with energy.

Charlie left and Alice sat on the end of the bed which was really soft and she sank deep into it, so kicking off her shoes she scooted up the bed, curled up on her side and closed her eyes and fell asleep to the sound of gentle laughter and of people moving around outside. It was so cosy she dropped off quickly.

What seemed like hours later, she felt Charlie sit down on the side of the bed next to her, and she began to softly stroke the side of her face as she opened her eyes.

'God I was out for the count, how long was I asleep?'

'About an hour, not long. Feel better for it?'

'Think so, didn't realise how tired I was until we set off.'

'Well don't worry about a thing, Jen and I have sorted stuff out, lunch is ready if you want to join us on a log?'

Alice stretched and sat up slowly. 'You are wonderful you know.'

'Nah, I just like taking care of you love. Need a hand?'

'Can you see my shoes anywhere?'

Charlie stood and looked around, retrieved them from the floor at the foot of the bed and passed them over. Alice slid her feet into them and they headed outside where a picnic table and chairs, along with tablecloth was set up outside.

'There just had to be a tablecloth didn't there?' smiled Alice.

'Of course, not going to drop standards just because we're in a field,' laughed Charlie.

To one side of the camping area was another smaller table with a camping stove and 4 plates all filled with food. Jen carried paper plates over and set them down.

'What have we got here then? Is it the 1970s? Did I go to sleep and time went backwards?' said Alice looking down at her plate which contained Spam, beans and a baked potato.

'You can't go camping and not have some Spam,' said Jen laughing. 'Didn't slice me finger off either undoing the bugger so it's win win.'

'And how did you cook a jacket spud in an hour, in a field?'

'There's a spud wagon over there, so I cheated,' laughed Charlie. 'Hope you like it.'

'Of course, it's brilliant. Great idea and so funny, really takes me back' she said cutting a piece of Spam and eating it. 'Mmmm it's just like I remember.'

'Is that a good or a bad thing?' smiled Charlie. 'Dig in everyone, and minimal washing up! Disposable plates, genius if I do say so myself.'

'Nowt wrong with your ego sis,' said Jen smirking across at Charlie.

After they'd eaten they all headed over towards where the music and events were happening, passing groups of women erecting small and large tents. Beyond them in the next field there was large stage set up surrounded by food and drink outlets. Lots of women had set up their picnic blankets and chairs near the front of the stage, so after a quick wander around to locate the loos and the shower block, they all sat on the grass and watched the first band play. The temperature was a perfect 20 degrees and the menopausal women in the field were visibly pleased.

A couple of hours later Holly got a text to say some of her friends from the doctors surgery she worked at had arrived, so she headed off to meet them after they all agreed to meet up later around the firepit.

Charlie lay on the grass, Alice's head on her chest listening to the music and tapping their feet, at one point nodding off in-between groups playing. Alice felt so relaxed and happy, and that she could face whatever lay ahead. At some point Jen had gone off to look around the site and returned with four ice creams with flakes in them, they had partially melted and were running down her arm.

'Hurry up sis, I'm getting covered,' said Jen handing two of the ice creams over.

'Cheers, just what the doctor ordered.'

'No sign of Holly?' asked Jen her eyes sweeping the field, desperately trying to get control over the quickly melting ice creams.

'Not since she got the text, she's probably just catching up with her colleagues,' said Alice glancing sideways at Charlie who turned her head away.

'Yeah, gonna drop her a text,' said Jen handing the ice creams over to Charlie. Then realising how sticky her hands were, she took them back again. 'Might as well have these first, I'm sure she's fine. I can always go and buy her another when she comes back'

They ate and made 'yum' noises, there was nothing quite like an ice cream on a warm summers day. Jen ate her two quicker than the others ate their solo offerings. But that was just Jen, a bottomless pit who never put an ounce of weight on.

After a further half hour there was still no sign of Holly, Jen caught Alice checking her phone again, she'd done that a few times that afternoon which was odd as she wasn't an addict with her phone like most of the women she knew.

'What cha doing?' asked Jen. 'Summat up?'

'Not exactly, but we need to go back to the tents, Holly is waiting for us there. No questions ok,' said Alice smiling.

Jen opened her mouth to speak then closed it with a puzzled look on her face as they all packed the picnic things away and headed back across the field. As they got closer to their tents Jen spotted a crowd, and as they got closer she realised it was Holly's surgery friends and her best friend from school Sarah who lived down in Wiltshire.

'What are you ....,' she began to ask.

Sarah came over and hugged them all. 'Hey, you're looking well Jen, business good?'

'Yeah good........... what's going on? Didn't know you were coming up?'

'Well it's a surprise. I'm guessing this is Charlie and Alice?' she said looking at the pair.

'God, sorry. Yeah. This is my sis Charlie and her partner Alice. This is Sarah, Holly's best mate from school. Now will someone tell me what's happening?'

Charlie cleared her throat. 'Alice, do you want to, you know.'

Alice smile beamed from ear to ear and hugging Jen who looked very confused, she headed into Holly's tent.

'Should I be worried?'

'Not at all, anyway here's Holly now.'

Jen turned towards their tent as the flap opened and Holly dressed in a white flowered dress with a band of flowers in her blonde hair, carrying a bunch of cream roses and purple wildflowers to match the ones in her hair. She was accompanied by Jen and Charlie's mum Madeline, who walked over and joined them.

Jen stood, her mouth agape. 'Holly, you look amazing, is this what I think it is? Mum?'

Before she could ask any further questions Holly went down on one knee. 'Darling Jen, I know we've talked of getting married, but life has got in the way a bit. I wanted today to be about us. It's the anniversary of the day we had our first date, so I've arranged for us to have a hand fasting in the woods. I love you, and I want to share today with our closest friends and family. Your mum is here too, she wouldn't miss it for the world. So Jen, my slightly bonkers partner, will you marry me?'

Jen, her eyes welling up scooped Holly up, hugging her tightly, 'Of course lass, you're amazing you know. But just one question. What am I wearing, I'm guessing you've been plotting that too?'

There was a massive cheer from their friends, and people walking over the field joined in too.

Holly laughed, she'd been plotting with Charlie and Alice for the past couple of months what was going to happen, and because entertainment was Charlie's bag, she knew that all would be great and like clockwork.

'Charlie has a couple of outfits for you to choose from, but if you wanted to go as you are that's ok too,' said Holly, she knew that dressing up really wasn't Jen's thing.

'Lead the way sis, let's get me married,' Jen said beaming from ear to ear, following Charlie into her tent.

As they got inside she was met by everything laid out on the bed. 'Let's freshen up at the shower block, I've got your wash bag and towel,' said Charlie.

So off they went to get ready, Jen with the biggest smile as she practically skipped across the field, Charlie hurrying to catch up.

Alice hugged Holly and Madeline. 'Phew, I didn't think I could keep quiet about it for much longer, I have been fit to burst about it. Charlie's had to keep reminding me to stop smiling so much. How are you Madeline?' she asked turning to see the petite French woman who was mother to the two extraordinary women in her life.

'Very good, you will marry Charlie soon?' she said with the same cheeky grin of her daughters.

'We will I'm sure one day and you'll be our guest of honour there too,' she replied. They were engaged and had talked about marriage but were waiting until the time was right.

'Sometimes life is too short for waiting. If it feels right you should grasp it with both hands my darlings,' she said taking hold of Holly and Alice's fingers. 'If you find love hold onto it, embrace it. Love is the greatest feeling of all.'

Madeline dabbed her eyes with her handkerchief, clearly moved.

A short while later Jen and Charlie returned, going into the tent to change then came out wearing matching cream linen suits.

Alice ducked into their tent and put on the pale blue linen dress and matching flat powder blue shoes that she'd brought with her to wear. Charlie had also arranged for the florist to leave buttonholes and flowers at the entrance to the wood where the ceremony was being held, and the caterers would be arriving very soon to set up. She was so excited for them, she did love a wedding.

Coming out of the tent she found the wedding party all waiting at the entrance to the woods. Charlie had found the flowers and they were all wearing either white roses with a hint of wild lavender buttonholes or corsages.

Walking to the entrance of the woods with Alice on her arm, they led the wedding party down the tree lined path towards the ceremony.

Chapter Two – To dance by candlelight

It was magical. The pathway was lined with fairy lights, but even though it was still daylight, as they got deeper into the forest the canopy of trees shielded out the sun and it got darker and darker. As they neared the centre of the woods there was a large clearing with two sets of chairs with a central clear path for the aisle. At the head of the aisle was an arch of flowers which had grown over a wooden gazebo. The aisle was strewn with rose petals and the rows of chairs all had white cloth covers with lilac sashes. Lanterns lined the route down the aisle and at the head stood a celebrant with a large white book waiting.

The guests took their seats and Charlie kissed Alice and went and took her place on the front row.

Alice joined Holly as she was going to walk her down the aisle, Madeline took Jen's arm.

'I would be honoured to walk you down the aisle Genevieve if you allow?'

Jen took her mums arm. 'Thanks mum,' she was clearly moved.

From behind them they heard someone running through the trees, turning they saw Grace heading their way. She and Holly had met at medical school and been friends ever since.

'Sorry I'm late. Congratulations to you both,' she said rushing to take a seat at the front next to Charlie.

Suddenly music started playing from speakers hidden in the trees.

'This is me. See you down there,' said Holly grinning at Jen, as she and Alice slowly walked through the trees and down the aisle to 'Eternal Flame' by the Bangles.

As the music stopped it was replaced with the music for Jen, picked out especially for her, a record that had been a favourite when they first started dating back in the late 1980's. Holly had chosen the Fine Young Cannibals 'She drives me crazy', a song that had meant such a lot to them when they were both fresh from coming out, and became estranged from their parents. Jen had only recently sorted out the differences with Madeline and many bridges had been repaired over the past year. It had all come about when Charlie traced her birth mother Madeline, and then found out that Jen was her half-sister as well as being Alice's best friend. It had been one hell of a year.

As Jen and Madeline walked to the top of the aisle Holly was there waiting, the biggest smile on her face and her eyes twinkling.

The officiant stepped forward.

'Welcome all. I'm Amanda and I'll be conducting this hand fasting ceremony for Holly and Jen. This is a beautiful day and a place to join together these women, in celebration of their deep love and affection, and to show to everyone just how important they are to each other.'

Jen and Holly stood holding hands facing each other, from the cheeky grin on Jen's face the crowd knew she was dying to crack a joke but was holding back. The joy on her face however was clear to see.

Amanda stepped forward carrying a long purple ribbon with cream tassels on each end. 'Can you hold each other's hands furthest away from me,' she requested and the two women dropped the one nearest as the celebrant draped the ribbon over their clasped hands.

Amanda continued. 'Handfasting is a promise about feelings from one person to another. It's one of the world's oldest wedding traditions and used in many cultures around the world. In joining hands, Jen and Holly are symbolising how they freely offer their lives to one another. And in fastening their hands together, the ribbon symbolizes how Jen and Holly will leave this place with lives now bound together. Their two stories have come together with two sets of hopes and desires for the future, as they are joined in both commitment and intention,' Amanda paused as she tied the ribbon together, binding their hands together.

'Jen and Holly, as I fasten your hands together and tie the knot, I invite you to reflect on the joy and responsibility that awaits you. From today, being bound together in the commitment and intention of marriage means that each of you both have a lifelong, safe place to love and be deeply loved by the other. Do you have any vows you would like to exchange?'

Holly nodded.

'Then please share them with Jen before all your friends.'

Holly took her free hand and within the folds of the skirt of her dress she pulled out a card. 'My darling Jen. Firstly thanks for not freaking out and doing a runner! We have shared such a long time together and created so many memories over the years. We've had our shares of good and the bad, happy and sad, but we have stood strong against the tides that have pushed and pulled us together and apart. I will always encourage and share your dreams because they are my dreams too. In a thousand different lifetimes I would always choose you to be by my side. You are my one, my only and like the song, my Eternal Flame. I love you from the bottom of my heart and this poem by Wendy Cope reflects the words I want to say to you.'

I cannot promise never to be angry;
I cannot promise always to be kind.
You know what you are taking on, my darling –
It's only at the start that love is blind.
And yet I'm still the one you want to be with
And you're the one for me – of that I'm sure.
You are my closest friend, my favourite person,
The lover and the home I've waited for.
I cannot promise that I will deserve you
From this day on. I hope to pass that test.

I love you and I want to make you happy.
I promise I will do my very best.

Jen's eyes had welled up and Holly could tell she was trying her best to hold it together.

'Would you like to say a few words Jen, I know this has all been a surprise to you.'

Jen tried as hard as she could to compose herself. 'Holly, you know I'm not the sloppy, sentimental type, and your words choked me, it's not often I'm lost for words which I am now. We've been through stuff you and I; it's been a blast. You've made today so special, as special as the last thirty odd years have been. I wouldn't have wanted to do it with anyone else. You've supported me through everything, loved me when I've been an arse and shown such kindness when I've messed up. I just want to say how much I love you. You know I'm not one for poems and such, but yours was cracking. Thanks love.'

Jen leaned over and kissed Holly. 'Shit, sorry was that allowed?' she asked.

The whole congregation howled with laughter.

'You're free to do whatever you like Jen, this is your day,' said Amanda. 'Would you like to say anything else?'

Jen visibly blushed, not something she usually did. 'No, I'm all good, that ok Holls?'

Holly smiled and nodded.

Amanda looped the ribbon twice around their hands and tied it underneath.

'Jen and Holly, remember always that together in this marriage, you are each deeply loved. And now, with great joy in front of all your closest friends and family, by the authority given to me, I pronounce you wives together. You can now kiss your bride Jen.'

Everyone was laughing, crying and on their feet clapping.

Jen and Holly turned and walked back down the aisle warmly greeted by their friends and family who hugged them as they passed along the line.

Once they were all out of the clearing and got back to the tents it was just getting dark and there were a million stars shining down on them from the clear sky. Holly led the way through a gateway and into a field beyond where there was a small marquee set up with tables laid out and a buffet spread out on a table. To Jen's delight it included heated trays of sausages and bacon her favourite.

'Wow, you really thought of everything,' said Jen helping herself.

'Not me love, the catering and arrangements were all Charlie and Alice. They know you well sweetheart.'

'Cheers sis,' she said her mouth full and wielding a sausage on a fork. 'Tuck in everyone, happy handfasting day to us!'

The guests all mingled around the food, taking plates to laid out tables but with no named seating so anyone could sit wherever they liked on golden chairs. Grace sat with Alice and Charlie who looked tired. They hadn't seen her for a few weeks because of her workload at the hospital.

Jen and Holly, all smiles, came and sat with them too.

'Congratulations to you both, thank you for inviting me too,' said Grace eating a tuna vol-au vent.

'I wanted you there, you're one of my oldest friends. The fun we had at medical school and sharing our first flat. You were a key part of the beginnings of me and Jen. Thank you for all your support over the years,' said Holly giving her a hug.

Grace visibly blushed, and as a distraction said, 'So what are your plans now? Are you going to get legally married too?'

'We've talked about that before and we will, but think it'll just be us two and maybe a couple of witnesses, that part isn't as important to us. Legally we need it, should anything happen to one of us, but it's just a formality.'

'Fair enough, that's a good plan. What about a honeymoon? Hope you'll at least take one of those?'

'Funny you should say that, and glad you're all here. We wondered if we could all go away somewhere together, to celebrate today properly and celebrate Alice's new book. What do you think?' suggested Holly.

Jen enthusiastically nodded her approval, her mouth full of bacon sandwich.

'Great idea,' said Charlie. 'I wanted to do something but wasn't sure what, getting published and all that. It's big.'

'Don't be daft, you don't have to do that for me,' said Alice going red in the cheeks. 'It's nothing special.....'

Holly cut her off.

'It's very special indeed, you've written a brilliant book. It has to be celebrated.'

'Oooo Holly, that was hot!' said Jen putting her hand around her waist and pulling her close to kiss her neck.

'Get a room,' sang the chorus round the table.

They all laughed, it was normally everyone saying it to Charlie and Alice, it made a change to say it to someone different.

'I think we should all go away somewhere, and fairly soon. If we can get holiday from work? Charlie being her own boss is the only one who is the freer spirit.' Said Holly.

'I've always wanted to go to see the Parsonage at Haworth and do nice visits to places around there. Anne Lister was from near there. We could do a lesbian tour! And the Tod disco too, how brilliant would that be, rent a cottage or something,' said Alice excitedly.

'Ace,' said Charlie. ' Sounds a great plan. Shall I get some details together?'

'You're the planner so if you could and wouldn't mind?' said Holly.

'Leave it with me, you know I like a project!'

'You certainly do,' said Alice. 'One of the many reasons we love you.'

'Shucks. You'll have me blushing next. Have you both had a great day? Did we do good?'

'Brill sis. A lovely surprise, love the outfits by the way. Very stylish.'

'Cool, glad you liked it. Anyone fancy going to listen to the last bands playing? Finish the night off?'

'I'm up for that, anyone fancy a dance? I want a dance with my beautiful wifey' said Jen reaching out her hand to Holly.

A resounding yes went round the group, so as soon as the food was finished they all headed over to the next field where the bands were playing their final sets. There they danced the night away without a care in the world.

Chapter Three – Heart breaker

Squinting against the daylight that streamed into her living room, Grace attempted to open her eyes. She was so tired after falling asleep on the sofa yet again, her body crumpled, tucked up in a ball for warmth and attempted comfort. It had been a rough night.

She'd got in from work around 11 the previous night after having a particularly difficult patient as the team had struggled to stabilise her. Grace had only left when her colleague told her to go and she'd take over, but once home she couldn't settle. Lots of patients came and went through her consulting rooms and operating theatre after surgery, but this woman had been different.

She'd come onto the presurgical ward from A&E for a stent to be fitted. Grace had come down for final checks on her surgeries that day, confirming what she'd do, and then answered any concerns from the patient. Most of the time there was a supportive partner or relative with them, however on this occasion the woman had been alone and terrified after a heart attack the previous day. After scans and tests it had been decided that she needed two stents inserting to prevent a further episode and any further heart damage.

Grace had spotted her as soon as she got onto the side ward which had five beds, four of which were empty. Her patient was laid on her side, drip in her arm, her body curled up tight, staring straight ahead of her and seemed unaware of her approaching.

Of course there was always a high level of anxiety for patients awaiting any operation, but experience immediately showed her that this patient was different, the level of pain emitting from her was emotional, not physical.

Taking the clipboard from the end of the bed Grace checked she had the right patient.

'Hi Juliette, I'm Dr Star. I understand that Dr Lowe has explained the procedure to you?'

The woman nodded, still not looking at her.

'Is there anything you want to ask before we take you into surgery? Anyone you need to call or is there anyone here with you?' she asked looking at the empty chair and no sign of a visitor.

Her patient shook her head and burst into tears; large blobs appeared on the pillow as they streamed down her face.

'I understand this is really scary but we do these operations every day, and in all likelihood you'll be able to go home today if not tomorrow,' explained Grace, Juliette all the while stared at the wall. 'Is there anyone you want to call before we take you to theatre, you're scheduled to go in about an hour. You won't be able to drive for a week so you'll need to arrange transport home.'

She sobbed loudly. 'She just left me.'

'Who left you?' asked Grace taking a seat at the side of the bed, making eye contact with her for the first time.

The woman in the bed jumped slightly as she looked at the rainbow lanyard around Grace's neck.

Juliette paused then said, 'My girlfriend broke up with me yesterday.'

'I'm sorry to hear that. Is there anyone we could call for you?'

'I haven't told anyone what's happened…………..can't believe it.' Suddenly her tone changed. 'Could I die?'

'There's a risk with any operation, but having a stent fitted is a simple procedure and you're in good hands, but you shouldn't be alone afterwards. Have you got a phone to ring someone?'

She nodded, indicating to Grace that her phone was on the bedside cabinet. Grace picked it up and passed it to her.

'Do you want me to make the call?'

Juliette shook her head.

'OK I'll leave you to make your call, I'm so sorry about your news, just try and relax, we won't be long as you're first on my list today.'

Grace walked out of the ward and spoke to the Sister about keeping a close eye on Juliette, before going up to the theatre so she could prep for the mornings operations. She pondered over her patients problem; it was awful how someone's life could change overnight.

Juliette's was the first surgery of the morning, everything was prepped to perfection and the operation had gone like clockwork, but in recovery they'd struggled to stabilise her BP, and at one point they nearly took her back to theatre. However after some time they managed to stabilise her.

After a long day in theatre Grace went to check on her patients before she went home, Juliette was still heavily sedated and wouldn't be going home that night. There had been no visitors. She noticed her phone on the cabinet flashing a couple of times whilst she checked her obs and thought that she would hopefully have someone in to see her the following day.

She sat in the nurses station, helping do observations until she went home when all seemed quiet. Most of the patients who'd had surgery that day had already gone home, others would be out in the morning after rounds including Juliette. So feeling reassured she left the ward.

Immediately upon waking Grace called her colleague to get an update on her patients, everything ached so whilst the phone rang she hunted for pills and put the kettle on.

She lived in the annexe behind her parents manor house in Askham Bryan, with an open plan kitchen/dining room/living room, it was all very modern with the original beams adding a bit of character. She loved her little house. She'd moved back after the breakup of her relationship with her long-term girlfriend, someone she thought she would spend the rest of her life with.

The phone was answered at the other end.

'Hi, it's Dr Star, I'm just calling to check in on one of my patients Juliette Smith, could you check for me?'

'Of course, just hold the line and I'll get the Sister.' Came the reply.

There was the noise of low voices, footsteps and the squeak of a trolley wheel as Grace sat waiting for the ward Sister.

'Morning Dr Star, its Staff Nurse Holland, how can I help?'

'I'm just calling for an update on Juliette Smith, is she ready to discharge this morning?'

There was silence down the phone.

'I'm sorry, she crashed about 5am, we worked on her but I'm sorry but we couldn't bring her back.'

Grace was silent. It was rare to lose a patient, and each one hurt because of the sense of failure, but this one hit hard.

'Ok thanks for letting me know, I'll be in shortly.' And with that she hung up.

After a quick shower she was out of the door and on her way to the hospital, it was earlier than normal and she was there in no time and had many car parking spaces to choose from in the normally rammed staff carpark. She made her way up to the ward, the senior consultant would be in for the team debrief, and there would be a postmortem to find out the cause of death. It would be an anxious wait to find out whether she'd missed something during the surgery, or if there was another cause.

The ward Sister gave her a small smile of greeting and passed her Juliettes' notes. Grace sat down at the nurses station going through it all meticulously. There wasn't anything there out of the ordinary, the drugs that were given to revive her were exactly what she would have done, she was stunned what could have happened.

'Were you there with her?' Grace asked the ward Sister.

'Yes, we did everything by the book, she was really upset prior to it happening, she was groggy from the procedure still but had had a phone call with someone, she was crying, then she dropped the phone and that was it she crashed.'

'I see, thanks for letting me know. I'll wait for the team meeting and then get back home; I'm supposed to be on leave but I just…..'

'I get it. Go get yourself a drink and see you in the meeting soon.'

'Have you contacted her next of kin? Were there any in the notes?'

'Yes there was the number of her mother and her girlfriend, we got through to her mother who has the details of what to do next, she was so shocked, she'd no idea she was in hospital.'

'Juliette told me that her girlfriend had broken up with her the day before, I guess she doesn't need to know now.'

'Very true. Poor lass, she was really distraught.'

Grace headed to the staff room and made a cup of coffee, took her notepad from her locker and headed to the team meeting down the corridor. The meeting was quick, each gave an account of what had happened in the surgery, the secretary took notes, the staff on the ward then gave theirs, and they agreed to be contacted with further questions if necessary after the postmortem.

After the meeting Grace headed to say goodbye to the duty staff at the desk. An elderly woman was there talking to the staff nurse.

'Dr Star this is Juliette Smith's mother, she's just come to collect her things.'

'I'm so sorry for your loss,' said Grace feeling awkward.

'The nurse was telling me they did all they could, I didn't even know she was ill. We'd not spoken in a while.'

'I'm sorry to hear that.'

'How was she, besides the heart thing?'

'I saw her before the operation and she was upset, she'd just broken up with her girlfriend and was distressed.'

'Juliette broke up with her?' asked the mother.

'No, Juliette said that the girlfriend broke up with her.'

'Sounds about right to me, caused no end of problems she did. She's the reason I hadn't seen her for months. Wish she'd called me yesterday; I hate to think of her being alone.'

'There were staff with her at the end but I know what you mean. I am so sorry. We'll know more soon and we'll be in touch.'

'Thanks doctor. For everything.'

Walking back to her car Grace reflected on what had happened. This wasn't the first time she'd lost a patient; each had their own sadnesses, but seeing how upset she had been had hit her hard. She remembered how devastated she'd been after her own break up.

Three years prior her long-term relationship had ended after her girlfriend Linda, (a fellow doctor) who she'd been living with for ten years, decided to emigrate to Australia for a better quality of life and a far improved salary. It had hurt for a long time and she'd sworn herself off meeting anyone else. But watching her friends pair up, get married and have children really hurt and she quietly confessed in her journal that she felt lonely. Juliette's sadness had really hit her.

She hated dating and initially the idea of putting her heart on the line again filled her with dread. So many of her friends had found love and were happily settling down, and she knew that she had to take the risk if she was to ever find that same happiness.

However she was finding it increasingly hard to find women who wanted to commit beyond a couple of dates. The dating scene had changed since she was last young, free and single. She'd met all her previous girlfriends at parties or been introduced through friends. Oh how things had changed!

Everything was now online and consisted of left and right swiping, of likes, pokes and hearts, rarely progressing further than that. She'd tried this modern way of dating, swiping done on autopilot, knowing darn well that you cannot tell someone's personality just from a brief synopsis, from women who write the bare minimum to cover up their shyness. Her inbox had filled up with couples wanting threesomes, women asking odd questions within two messages, such as are you top, bottom or switch? Can I send you a nude?

However the cherry on the cake of online dating were the ghosters. The intriguing, intense flurry of messages which made her believe that she might actually have met a nice person, then suddenly they'd disappear off into the sunset, never to make contact ever again. Grace wondered whether she had appeared too keen or were these women dead on their sofa being eaten by their three cats.

It definitely seemed that older women were more cautious and battle scarred, not willing to open their hearts to the possibilities of finding true love and scarpering as soon as things got a little bit serious. You know, like wanting to exchange phone numbers.

So Grace knew that going back to online dating again lay ahead, there were so few places to meet women, even Valentines', an LGBT bar that Charlie owned had proved fruitless. Being a university town the clientele were very young so she was low on options. She also knew that she wasn't feeling the love of doing the quick step to avoid the fucked-up players intent on bringing their wrecking balls into her life from online dating. It was a vicious tightrope walk.

Seeing Juliette heartbroken really made her want to go stay home and hibernate.

As she pulled into the drive her dad waved from the garden, it was good to have them close most of the time, but today she needed head space to think, and for the first time in ages to reflect on how she had got to where she was now. Retrieving the suitcase of photographs and mementos from underneath the bed, she sat on the floor and opened it. It contained all the albums of adventures her and Linda had had in their time together, including a long trip to Brisbane where they'd enjoyed the lifestyle and touring in a motorhome for 6 months. It was that trip that convinced Linda to emigrate, but Grace knew she couldn't leave her elderly parents. It had broken her heart. Had that final phone call quite literally broken Juliette's too?

She hadn't looked at their photos since she'd packed them away when she left. Should she have just gone? It was all too late now, Linda had already met and married a fellow doctor in a lavish beach ceremony, how could she have moved on so quickly when she was still stuck in a vicious cycle of dating fear?

Suddenly her phone pinged knocking her out of her reverie.

'Hope you're packing, we'll be there to pick you up at 9 tomorrow morning, can't wait love Alice x'

Chapter Four – Moving on Up

'Shit.'

She'd totally forgotten about going away, so taking out her holdall she packed enough clothes for a few days, and of course with it being Yorkshire, she threw in a few jumpers too. She'd booked her leave at work, mainly because she had to use it up before the end of March, with everything going on she'd forgotten to pack. Since the camping trip Alice wouldn't let it lie that they all needed a break.

Alice and Charlie had become good friends, Lou her next-door neighbour had hung out with Alice when they were teenagers, playing horses and galloping around North Yorkshire randomly on a weekend.

She hadn't been looking forward to the holiday. Going away with two couples whilst she was firmly single was going to be hell she'd decided, and she wished to high heavens that she'd said no when she'd been asked.

'God why didn't I say NO!!'

'Get a grip Grace.'

She loved their company really. Holly was a fellow doctor and they'd gone through medical school at York together, and Jen her wife was an absolute spitfire, and a rather brilliant in-demand electrician. They always had such a hoot when they were together, it was just that after the past couple of days Grace didn't feel herself.

Ping Ping

It was a text from her mum. *'Darling, fancy coming over for dinner?'*

'Ok give me 10 mins.'

Once packed she headed over to her parents' house, the place she'd grown up in before going to boarding school. It was the largest in the village, the former Manor House which her mum had inherited it from her grandmother so it had been in the family for at least 150 years. It's pink/red bricks made it look as though it had come out of a romantic picture book. Especially today in the late summer sunshine, its tall Georgian sash windows partially open. She let herself in the back door taking off her shoes before being greeted by her parents black labrador Maisie who came waddling down the passageway.

'How are you doing old girl,' she said bending down to give her a cuddle. Ahead she heard the clink of cutlery on plate and that was the cue Maisie needed to return to where the good stuff was happening.

'Hi mum,' said Grace giving her mum a kiss.

'You look tired love, hard day?'

'Just a bit. Need a hand?' she replied shutting down that line of questioning. She loved her parents but didn't want them worrying so she set about helping her mum set out dinner. They were very old school; dinners were formal affairs still with pots and dishes for everything laid out on the table in the middle of the dining room. Today it was salmon and vegetables with new potatoes and she spotted a trifle on the sideboard, her dads favourite.

Her parents had been married almost 70 years; how did you keep a relationship going that long? Maybe it was just lesbians who didn't have longevity.

'Darling!' announced her dad coming and hugging her. 'Has your mum told you our news?'

'No, I've just got here, what have you two got planned? Trip to the Amazon? Wrestling with crocodiles in Florida?' laughed Grace. Her parents had never been conventional.

Her dad laughed loudly.

'Don't be giving him ideas Grace, you know we nearly got lost last year in Morocco.'

'Please don't remind me! I nearly sent for International Rescue.'

They all sat at the large dining table decanting food onto the best China only brought out on special occasions.

'Ok, what's going on? Best cutlery and plates, are you expecting someone else? Is the vicar coming? The King?'

'No we had the vicar for tea yesterday,' smiled her mum with a cheeky glint in her eye. 'Your father and I have come to a decision; we've decided that it's time for us to downsize and live somewhere more suitable for us as we're not getting any younger. So we wondered how'd feel about swapping houses? Yours is all one level and I can see the stairs being an issue with my knees.'

'You could fit a stair lift?' said Grace helpfully.

'We could, but the upkeep of the house is getting a bit much, and we think it's time for you to put your stamp on the house. Give it some thought darling.'

'Of course. I do get it, and you know I love the house. Let me have a think about it for a bit. What are your other options? Sell up totally?'

'I don't think I could ever sell it, we've too much history here, but we have to make things easier, we're not getting any younger. But in saying that we've just booked to go away in the New Year on the Orient Express and then a cruise up the Nile, I fancied the full Agatha Christie experience.'

'You're both bonkers. It says something when my parents have a more exciting life than me.'

'You could come with us? Take some time out from work?'

'Maybe. Crikey you two, you've given me food for thought today! I'm going away with the girls this weekend, can I have a think and come for tea on Monday and we can chat about the house more?'

'Of course darling, take your time. Hope you have lots of fun.'

'Thanks dad,' said Grace as she helped clear the table and washed the plates whilst he dried, talking about their trip and past adventures including camel trekking in Egypt, climbing Mount Kilimanjaro twice and back packing around South America.

'Are you sure you wouldn't prefer a couple of weeks by the pool in an all-inclusive in Spain? That's what most parents do on their holidays.'

'That's not our thing darling, you've never had our sense of adventure have you?'

Grace shrugged her shoulders. 'Guess not, I'm a homebody at heart.'

Her dad gave her a brief hug. 'Don't fret, maybe after this trip we'll be ready to be sensible.'

'I somehow doubt that,' said Grace putting away the last plate in the cupboard. 'I'd better get going and make sure I've got everything sorted. See you when I get back, well that's unless you're not paddle boarding up the Nile by then.'

'Bye darling, have a lovely time, send us a postcard,' her mum said hugging her. 'Let us know you've got there ok.'

'Shall do, love you both,' she said heading for the door, giving Maisie a pat goodbye on her way out.

Returning to the annexe she double checked her bag, set her alarm and headed for bed hoping for a dreamless sleep and not the romantic dreams she'd been having lately. There was always a woman walking towards her through the mist, in her heart within the dream she knew they were in love, there was a deep connection, yet she never reached her, she was faceless and she disappeared, enveloped in the mist.

For god's sake, I can do without my brain making up women!

Chapter Five – The Wildness of the Moors

Grace regretted wishing away the nice dreams of love, instead she had another restless night with nightmares of being lost in hospital corridors, losing patients and being dragged screaming into a prison cell. As soon as dawn broke she got up and straight into a very hot shower hoping it would freshen her up.

After dressing and her first cup of strong coffee she saw her neighbour Lou heading to the stables opposite to sort out the horses. So grabbing her phone and keys she followed her into the yard. There were only a couple of horses in the stables, it had been a lovely warm summer and the grass was lush so most of them lived outside 24/7, only two had to come in overnight as they'd put so much weight on so they were on restricted rations.

She saw the tack room door open and heard the jangle of metal, so following the noise she shouted ahead so as not to startle her friend.

'Morning Lou, need a hand?' she asked

'Hey, couldn't you sleep either? This menopause lark is bloody hideous, one minute I'm boiling the next I'm freezing. I'm driving Henry mad with the covers on and off all night,' Lou said with a laugh. Menopause chats were regular within the group, they were all women of a certain age.

'Isn't it funny that one day we're discussing careers and nights out, now we're comparing HRT drugs and hot flushes,' laughed Grace feeling her worries lifting slightly. Being around horses and Lou always helped her to relax. 'Need a hand turning out?'

'That'd be helpful thanks,' she replied, handing a leather headcollar and burgundy lead rope to Grace. 'Can you take Harvey and I'll get Max?'

Grace nodded going to the stable to get the black and white gentle giant. Lou joined her with Max and they walked slowly down to the field, the horses still sleepy as they plodded behind. As they got nearer the field gate they perked up and picked up the pace, the joy of seeing their field mates and the chance of some lush grass making them keen.

Lou opened the gate and they all walked through, latching it again. Releasing their charges the horses gave little squeals and trotted off shouting to their field mates.

'Fancy a walk to check them all over? Just in case one of them has done something silly overnight?'

Looking at her phone screen which showed it was just after 7am, she had plenty of time before getting picked up by Charlie and her other friends.

'Sure, did I tell you I was away this weekend? I'd totally forgotten,'

'Alice told me you're all going on a lesbian themed break, I asked if I could be an honorary lesbian,' laughed Lou checking the horses over, none of whom were interested in them at all. 'It sounds amazing.'

'I'll be glad to get away, it's been a rough week.'

'You work too hard Grace; hope you can relax a bit.'

'Me too. I had dinner with Mum and dad last night and they want to downsize and swap houses, not sure I want to take on such a big house alone. Work is exhausting me too, maybe it's time to cut back and have a change of pace?'

'That's just how Henry felt before we left London, he was burnt out, it sounds like you are too lovie. If you want to talk properly come over when you get back, I'm sure Henry can help, or maybe Charlie, she's always got a ton of new ideas. Maybe a change would do you good Grace.'

'Perhaps. I've never really had a proper break. Other than the trip to Australia four years ago I've not really freed myself mentally, know what I mean,' shrugged Grace.

'I understand, I do. Henry will too.'

'I guess so. I better go and get ready for the girls. We're back Sunday if you're around in the afternoon?'

'Should be, just message, I'm sure we're around.'

'Thanks Lou,' she said giving her a hug. 'Have a nice weekend.'

The gang arrived at 9 on the dot, Charlie was a lovely woman but she was often like a sergeant major with her organisation of people and events. Today was no different. The boot of her Jeep Cherokee was packed with precision and she slotted Grace's rucksack into the small space that was left. She waved at Jen and Holly who were going to drive in convoy to their destination of Haworth where they were renting a cottage for a few days. It was the end of summer, and Charlie and Alice were celebrating both the anniversary of when they got together, and the publishing of her book about the life story of Charlotte and Hester, taken from the love letters Alice had found under the floorboard at her house. They were also celebrating the official wedding of Jen and Holly. They'd quietly gone to the registry office one afternoon, and with the aid of a couple of strangers they'd asked on the street they had formally got married to make everything legal. It had been quite a year for them all.

So to celebrate, after much discussion and debate, they had all booked to explore the very lesbian areas of Hebden Bridge, Shibden Hall and to finish the trip with a night at the Todmorden Women's Disco.

Haworth, the village where they would be staying was steeped in history, famous for the Parsonage where the Bronte sisters had lived and wrote many of their stories. The cottage they were staying in was not far from there and the wild expanse of moorland.

Both cars arrived at the cottage at the same time and parked in front of it on a cobbled street. The cottage was stone built, with roses round the door, not unlike the house that Alice had lived in when she was married to Sally.

Charlie got out of the car first. 'Just breathe in that beautiful clean air,' she said inhaling deeply. 'It's so good to get away from York.'

'I have to agree with you there sis,' said Jen opening the boot and beginning to unload the bags. Alice, Holly and Grace unlocked the Hide A Key and let themselves into the cottage.

Holly was gobsmacked. 'Oh it's so beautiful, just look at that fireplace.'

Alice, who's eyes were too busy exploring every nook and cranny of the cottage, nodded. It all felt familiar to her. Going into the kitchen she saw a beautiful cream Aga which thankfully was turned off, but it still looked beautiful taking pride of place within the room, just like the one she had in her old kitchen when married to Sally. She started to feel sad at the memory of her old house but knew in her heart that it was in the past. Her life now was much fuller in fun and love than she had ever had in her old house.

She was broken out of her reverie………

'Oh we'll have tonnes of fun making food in here, well that's if Charlie lets us,' laughed Holly. 'It's so posh! There's even an electric oven,' she said opening the oven door then continued to poke around the kitchen looking in all the cupboards, cooing every time she saw something cute.

'It's stunning,' said Grace, I'm going up to look at the bedrooms. Unless you want first dibs?'

'No of course, help yourself, it's got 3 double bedrooms, choose which one you want,' said Alice. 'Are you OK Grace you haven't said much since we picked you up.'

'It's OK don't worry, just something at work.'

Grace took her rucksack and headed up the steep stairs. At the top there were three doors, each one leading to a bedroom, one ahead and one to the left and one to the right. Grace took the door ahead. It opened up into a large room painted in a pale pink, with a white wooden bed with pink bedding with the added bonus of an en suite shower room to the side. The large picture window overlooked a garden which was still in full bloom, an immaculate luscious lawn, and beyond the hedge at the top lay the moors which the Bronte sisters had written about in their novels. Just looking at the view she could feel the tension that had been surrounding her ease. Outside the scenery was an utterly different place from where they had travelled from. Although she lived in a quiet village, this felt totally different. Askham Bryan was neatly ordered and pretty with manicured gardens, here there was the contrast of the well-tended gardens and the wildness above, a place where you could truly lose yourself in.

Grace sighed; she felt lost herself. The past few days had really knocked the stuffing out of her and now her parents wanted her to swap houses. Taking on the big house with just herself to fill it made her feel sad. She had always dreamed of living in it with a family of her own, a wife and children, having parties and having their friends to stay. Big Christmas's. That boat had sailed now. She knew how lucky she was to have these options but it was a massive decision. She unpacked and headed into the shower hoping it might perk her up and make things seem clearer.

Downstairs Charlie was unpacking the food leaving ingredients on the side which she'd planned to make supper with. She loved to entertain, after all that was what her job had been for so many years running restaurants and bars until she had built a little empire of her own. Alice watched her whilst making cups of tea, it'd been an amazing year.

It had all started with passion and love, but with a massive chunk of heartache after Charlie had cheated. That was when she'd reached rock bottom and sought help for her alcohol addiction. Her recovery went hand in hand with the reconciliation with Alice, a love that had blossomed over the past year.

'Penny for your thoughts?' said Charlie.

'Do you really want to know what I was thinking,' said Alice in her best sultry voice.

'Always', replied Charlie, smiling, a cheeky glint in her eye.

'Hey you two, we're here too,' said Jen laughing. 'Get a room.'

'Good plan, let's take our bags up, leave the love birds to flirt,' said Holly.

'Cheeky! Race you sis,' said Charlie grabbing their bags as she ran to the foot of the stairs, closely followed by Jen.

'God, those two are like kids aren't they!' said Holly, 'It's hard to believe that they were at each other's throats most of the time last year.'

Alice smiled. 'They've come a long way haven't they. What a year!'

The previous year, as well as finding the love of her life in Alice, Charlie had found her birth mother and a half sister Jen, who was Alice's best friend. Jen had gone from being a very defensive friend to loving sister, a true turnaround from the many arguments and harsh words after Charlie had broken Alice's heart.

'I'll go supervise, Jen's idea of unpacking isn't mine,' joked Holly.

'Thanks, I'll just get the rest of the food packed away and I'll be up too.' Replied Alice putting the milk in the fridge and looking at the food itinerary that Charlie had prepared, she smiled knowing how she always made such an effort for everyone.

'Ping. Ping. Ping. Ping'

'Ping. Ping. Ping.'

Alice looked around looking from where the sound was coming from, and saw Grace's phone on the sideboard in the hall, so picking it up she headed upstairs, noticing from the lit-up screen a number of text messages, but she didn't read them.

'Grace?' she called out.

'In here,'

Alice followed the sound of the voice into the room where Grace was wearing a dressing gown, her hair wet after her shower.

'Your phone was pinging a lot,' she said handing it over.

'Thanks,' said Grace taking the phone and looking at the screen. A smile slowly appearing on her face.

'Oooo, now that's a nice smile, do tell,' said Alice smiling back at her.

'It's from an anaesthetist from work, she's just asking if I'm ok after yesterday and if I'd like to go out for a drink tonight,' Grace stood staring at her phone. 'Do you think it's a drink or a date?'

'Is she on our bus?'

'Yeah, I know she had a girlfriend last year as she brought her to a retirement do, maybe they broke up?'

'What's her name? What's she like?'

'Her name's Helen, she comes from somewhere in Leicestershire I think, she only joined the department last June so I don't know much.'

'Is she your type? Ooooo romance!' said Alice grinning.

'Romance? What have I missed?' said Charlie coming into the room with Jen.

'Ey up Holls, get yourself in here, there's gossip.'

Holly came, quick as a flash.

'What have I missed? Romance? Come on spill,' she said giggling. Holly was a sucker for a bit of gossip and romance.

Alice was overkeen to share. 'Grace has been asked out by someone at work, what are you going to reply?'

'That's bloody brilliant,' said Jen. 'Go for it!'

'She's asked me out tonight but I'm not there am I? Bloody typical!'

'No, but it's the Tod women's disco tomorrow, get her to come over for that, less pressure?' suggested Alice.

'Should I? It's a lot to expect someone to drive all that way.' Said Grace.

'It's worth an ask. You never know, she might be coming anyway?' said Holly.

'Ok, I'll just reply and tell her all that, you lot are a bad influence!'

Grace began typing fast with both hands, her finger deleting words. 'God I can't type today.' She took a deep breath and started again.

'*Love is in the air,*' sang Jen and Charlie together. 'Snap.'

'Sometimes I preferred it when you two were fighting, come on let's get unpacked and leave Grace to set something up,' Holly said taking Jen's hand and taking her reluctantly out of the bedroom.

Charlie took Alice's hand, 'Let's unpack, the room is stunning, I might need a lie down,' she said winking at Alice.

Grace smiled following them to the door, closing it behind them, then set about replying to the text, legibly this time.

'*Hi Helen, thanks for the text, sorry I'm away on holiday in Haworth with friends. We're going to the Todmorden womens disco tomorrow night, do you want to come? Grace*'

She added and deleted an X at the end a couple of times, then decided against it. She put her phone down on the bed, stepping away from it like it was a dangerous weapon, her heart pounding. The dating game was a scary business.

Beginning to unpack she'd only filled half the top drawer when the phone pinged again.

Grabbing it off the bed she read the reply.

'I love Haworth, you lucky thing, I'm coming to Tod tomorrow night with some friends too, so see you there. H x'

Grace danced a little jig. She had a date! 'I have a date.' She shouted.

'Yippee's and Woo hoo's came from the other bedrooms.

She had a date, after all this time she had an actual date!

Chapter Six – In the footsteps of the Bronte's

After all the unpacking was done Charlie headed to the kitchen to prepare some lunch for them all before they headed out to look around the Parsonage. She knew Alice especially had been looking forward to going. She shouted everyone when she was finished and after quickly eating they all headed out.

Haworth village centre was still quaint despite the modernisation of the towns and cities around it, the stone-built houses and shops, the church, the cobbled streets, the very steep hill up to where the Parsonage sits near to the church where the Bronte's father was the vicar in the early 19th Century. The buildings almost unchanged except for the modern signage and the numbers of tourists.

Alice was giddy; she'd loved all things Bronte from being a teenager. The tragic but very brilliant sisters, Emily, Anne and Charlotte, their troubled brother Bramwell, and their father Patrick who served his parish for 41 years. Charlie loved to see her so happy and excited.

They all paid their entry fee and took the tour of the house, the rooms all staged as the Bronte's might have had them, the papers and books with their ancient handwriting upon them. Alice was all smiles. From Jen's face it was clear to see this really wasn't her thing.

'Would you mind if I went out for a wander? It's all a bit …… old for me' she asked.

'Of course not, I'll text you when we're done, have fun sweetie,' said Holly giving her a kiss.

'It's so quaint in here isn't it, but it must have been freezing in winter,' said Grace who was pleased of the distraction from their questions since Helen had confirmed their date tomorrow.

'Absolutely. The harshness of their life really came through in their writing though. Jane Eyre is my favourite.' Said Alice.

Both Grace and Holly nodded in agreement, Charlie, who wasn't a big reader gave an embarrassed grin. 'I liked the tv series.'

'Me too, the one with Ruth Wilson is my favourite,' said Grace.

'Oh yes, definitely. We ought to watch it together whilst we're here?' said Holly. 'Think that would be really cool.'

'Not sure Charlie and Jen would agree,' said Alice putting her arm round her. 'Would you mind?'

'Nah, I'll go get some nibbles in. See you when you've finished?'

'Ok love, see you soon. Go see if you can find Jen,' Alice said hugging her goodbye. 'I feel bad for suggesting all this historical stuff, sorry sweetheart.'

'Don't apologise, we're all here to toast your new book and we all want you to do stuff you enjoy, I'm just so bloody nervous I'll knock something over and cause an historical storm,' laughed Charlie. 'Everything is so tiny!'

After she'd left the three women toured the house, marvelling at the writing desks, Bramwell's untidy room and then they found the gift shop. Alice bought a few books, the Jane Eyre DVD they wanted to watch later and the obligatory postcards. Holly and Grace showed a little more restraint, but still came out with bags.

'I've just had a text from Charlie, she and Jen are in the tearoom down the hill, shall we go get a cup of something?'

There were two nods. So having paid they headed off to join them. It was thirsty work sightseeing obviously.

The streets of Haworth were crowded despite it being late in the summer season, thankfully it hadn't rained so the cobbles weren't slippery as they walked down the hill, past the church, and a shop called The Souk.

'We must have a look in there on our way back,' said Alice, 'It looks my kind of place.'

'Oh yes, I love an antique shop, though Jen will probably kill me if I buy anything,' said Holly.

The tea shop was very quaint with pale blue spotted tablecloths, painted white chairs and cake stands laid out with a multitude of cream cakes and other goodies. Jen and Charlie were tucking into a vanilla slice each, and a big pot of tea.

Alice went to the counter and ordered three cups of tea; they were far too full to want anything else. They were served quickly, and Alice also purchased yet more postcards of the village and the Parsonage.

'Sorry if we were a bit long,' said Alice.

'Did you enjoy yourselves?' Charlie asked. 'I felt like a giant in there, I was terrified of breaking something.'

'It's OK love I know it's not your thing, I do appreciate your coming and seeing what you did. Have you had fun?'

'Yeah we went into the place called the Apothecary, you'd love it Alice. It's really old fashioned.'

'What are you trying to say?' said Alice smiling, pretending to be insulted.

'I didn't mean it like that,' said Charlie smiling. 'But all the furniture in there is ancient. You almost expect Agatha Christie to walk into the shop. I got some nice smellies in these little bottles,' she said getting them out of the bag she had by her feet.

'Ooo I love them, glad you had fun darling,' she said kissing her.

'Talking of Agatha Christie, my parents have announced they're going on the Orient Express and then on a boat tour down the Nile, they are going full on Agatha aren't they!. They're in their late 80's and they have a far more exciting life than I do. They've invited me to go with them. Those are trips you aim to do as a couple, not with your parents!' said Grace sadly.

'That would be brilliant though, maybe you should go with them, what an adventure! exclaimed Holly.

'Besides the fact I don't want to go on a romantic holiday with my parents, I doubt it's my kind of thing. But how amazing they are. They have so much get up and go. I feel like mines got up and gone most days.'

'I know what you mean, I'm jiggered, the other day I woke up convinced it was the weekend, felt so pissed off when I realised it was Monday and I was starting a full rewire. How many hours a week do you work Grace? enquired Jen.

It varies, sometimes it's 40, sometimes it's 60, it just depends on how many emergencies I get in a week. I've been feeling so disheartened over the last few weeks, like I wasn't making a difference, that maybe it's time for a change.'

'What else would you like to do?' asked Charlie.

'I just don't know. I don't know what I want to do anymore. Medicine has been my life since I was 18. I don't know what else there is in life for me to do. I could take early retirement; I would have a decent pension but what would I do with my time?'

'What about volunteering abroad? Could you do that?' asked Holly.

'I just don't know if they'd want me. I've had such a horrible week at work, I'm not sure if I just want to leave the profession behind. Do something completely new. I have other news too,' announced Grace.

'OK so besides you're hating your job, your parents jetting off on an adventure, and having a date tomorrow what on earth else could there be?' Said Alice smiling.

'My parents want to swap houses. They want to move into the annex as they're finding the big house too much for them and they want me to take it over. It's been in the family for generations. I don't know what to do. I'd always imagined I would move into it with my own family one day, that I'd have children with a partner to fill the house with laughter like it was when I was a child. It seems such a waste for just me to be rattling around in it. I know how ungrateful I sound.'

'Hell! What a fucking choice,' said Jen. 'I'd take it with both hands, why not? It's what most people dream of. The big beautiful house in the country.'

'I know I'm so lucky, I know I am, but it's a massive decision. If I retire can I even afford to keep the house? It costs a small fortune to heat and the roof will probably need doing at some point.'

'Well maybe this new woman and you could move into it together? Said Jen.

'We haven't even had our first date yet! And you've got us married off!'

'Well, there's no point hanging around at our age is there. Go for it, if she makes you happy that is.'

'Well Jen I will do my best, you're bloody hilarious.'

'I try me best.'

After they had finished their tea, they headed across the road to the shop called The Souk. Alice and Holly were like children in a toy shop, Jen and Charlie stood at the door holding the bags like 2 disgruntled husbands.

'Come on then let's get back to the cottage whilst we've still got some space in the car to get home. I want to get on with dinner, I can hear Jen's stomach growling from here,' laughed Charlie.

'Very funny, it's just a few bits of China and a couple of cushions. Perhaps we could get something for the bedroom in your house,' suggested Alice.

'What's wrong with my bedroom? I don't hear you complaining about being in there usually,' said Charlie smiling.

Alice blushed, 'I just meant it needed a bit of softening up, it's a bit stark in there.'

'I prefer your bedroom anyway, it smells of you,' she said smiling giving Alice a kiss.

'You make me melt Charlie.'

'Get a room,' said the group in unison.

Chapter Seven – The Shibden Hall Pilgrimage

After an evening of good food and a chunk of the Jane Eyre DVD, they didn't go to bed until after 1am, so the following morning they all woke late. Jen was the first up followed by Grace, and they got started on breakfast.

The smell of bacon soon filled the kitchen, drifting upstairs waking the other occupants, weary eyed they came downstairs in search of coffee and food.

'Thanks guys, smells amazing, what can I do?' asked Charlie.

'Nowt sis, sit down and chill, we've got this.'

Charlie wasn't used to this; she took a seat at the table joined by Alice and Holly.

'Could get used to this, waitress can I get some coffee?' laughed Charlie snapping her fingers in the air.

'Certainly,' said Grace as she poured some coffee into mugs from the cafetiere and put them onto the table. 'Anyone want any juice?'

There was a resounding no as Jen served up the food, so after lots of chatter about their plans for the day Alice and Holly loaded the dishwasher and Charlie cleaned the kitchen.

'God I'm nervous about tonight! What if Helen was just being friendly?' said Grace looking stressed.

'Well maybe she was, but maybe she wasn't and really likes you, it'll be loads of fun whatever happens.' said Holly.

Grace didn't look convinced at all.

'Even if you don't end up a couple she obviously wants to be friends, and you never know she might have a single friend who you do like.'

'Maybe. I shouldn't be this nervous as a woman in her 50's should I,' smiled Grace.

'It's scary at any age lovely, it'll be ok, we're going to be there too so you're not alone.'

'Not sure that is a good thing,' laughed Grace. 'Ok I'm going to get showered, what time are we setting off for Shibden?'

'Eleven I think, gives us half an hour before Charlie starts shouting at us,' said Holly smiling over at Charlie who was looking at one of the books Alice had brought with her the previous day.

'Very funny, ok let's get ready and get this show on the road.'

Half an hour later they were all ready and in the car on the road to Shibden Hall, the old home of Anne Lister, the most well-known 19th century lesbian, whose amazing life and many loves were all written out in code in her spectacular diaries. It was another place that was high on Alice's list to visit, but was also a definite pilgrimage for any lesbian.

The drive there was scenic and full of twists and turns. Charlie's driving was calm and contained but she was noticeably very quiet. Alice put her hand on her leg as she drove.

'You ok sweetheart?' she asked quietly.

Charlie looked in the rear-view mirror where Jen, Holly and Grace were chattering away over a Tiktok on Jen's phone.

'Bit nervous about tonight to be honest.'

'Why love?'

'Well the old Charlie had a bit of a reputation at the Tod disco, so there's that.'

'Oh shit, I hadn't thought, we can always stay home if it'll be too hard.'

'Maybe it's just something I have to do, don't want to make you uncomfortable, to be honest I can't remember everything I did there over the years. Shit. Might just wear a placard saying I'm sorry if I was a bitch, might just save some time.'

'I'll be there sweetie, we'll face it together.'

'Just don't want to embarrass you love.'

'We're all here, we've got your back.'

Charlie held her hand and squeezed it before returning it to the wheel and turned the Jeep into the car park at Shibden Hall. 'Hope you're right.'

Shibden didn't disappoint, the house was so beautiful, situated on top of the hill looking down over a green valley. Inside was recreated how it would have been back in Anne Lister's day as much as was possible. Alice gave them a tour around from what she knew of the history, the grand hall, the four-poster bed with the top hat and the grandeur of the Jacobean style house. Jen, Charlie and Holly escaped after an hour and went down the hill to the café after their fill of seeing all the house had to offer.

Walking around the grand Jacobean house, Alice felt totally at home, not just because of the architecture, but also the inspiration from its former occupant Anne Lister. Her love of women at a time when women had no rights and were married off to regularly unsuitable men. Anne herself was no saint, many of her former lovers ended up in asylums after they had become involved with her, but the fact that she got to live her best life when most didn't, made her a heroine for many lesbians.

After exploring the house thoroughly they went outside to look at the old buildings and were beyond excited in the coach house where old bridles and saddlery were hung, including old carriages which had seen better days.

'You can almost imagine Anne Lister striding around here can't you, very atmospheric,' said Alice texting the trio to say they were finished with the house, only to get a text back saying the food was amazing and get themselves down to the café. So leaving the smell of leather and old hay behind them, they headed down to meet them.

'Is Charlie ok, she's been quite subdued,' asked Grace as they walked down the path towards the café and lake.

Alice told Grace of her concerns and what had happened way back when Charlie was living it up regularly when drunk, regularly picking up women at bars and disco's just for sex.

'It was ages ago, I'm sure it'll be ok, anyway we're here to support aren't we.'

'Yes, totally. 'Is everything ok with you, you mentioned something at work?'

'I can't say much but a patient I operated on died the morning after so I'm worried I missed something.'

'Bless you, I'm sorry, when will you find out?'

'There'll be a postmortem so after that I guess, it'll need a full investigation if it was something I missed, it was a sad case, I can't say anything else though.'

'I understand, I hope you find out quickly to ease your mind. I'm glad we're away together this weekend, hope that it helps, I can't imagine what you're going through. I know you quite literally hold the patient's life in your hands every day, that is such a lot of pressure Grace.'

'Thanks, it has been more of a strain lately I admit. I'm just weary I think. Being away is helping though so thanks for inviting me. I've just got to keep distracted until I know more.'

'We'll all help where we can,' said Alice opening the door to the café, and seeing their group sat at a table near the counter they went over.

It looked like Jen had already ordered one of everything off the menu, there were sandwiches and what looked like a chilli, an omelette and a couple of paninis.

'Were you feeling a bit peckish Jen?' asked Alice.

'It wasn't just me this time, Charlie's hungry too,' replied Jen with a cheeky grin.

Charlie attempted a similar smile but Alice could tell that it was very much put on, so she leaned over and kissed her on top of her head.

'Can we get anyone anything?' Alice asked.

The three at the table shook their heads helping themselves to the table feast.

'Advance warning, I'm making a big dinner before we go out tonight. Jen and I are cooking,' said Charlie.

'Thanks for the heads up.' Said Alice going to the counter with Grace and they only ordered a cup of tea and a piece of flapjack.

Once Jen and Charlie had finished hoovering what food there was on the assortment of plates they all headed off back up the hill through the parkland, the light breeze making the trees sing as they swayed gently. Looking back down the hill towards the lake they marvelled at the beauty of Anne's home and grounds, which were peaceful despite being so close to major cities.

Holly and Jen got into the back of the jeep with Grace, whilst Alice took the front passenger seat again, she suddenly felt very weary and in need of a nap. The steep hill climb had really taken it out of her, but she said nothing as she didn't want to spoil the mood, plus she told herself that they'd had a late night too, that was all it was. Nothing to worry about.

Chapter Eight – Dancing at Tod Disco

Returning to the cottage everyone but Charlie and Jen headed upstairs for naps or to read. Alice was knackered and crashed quickly. All the fresh air having done a good job of helping her to nod off. A couple of hours later Grace knocked on Alice's door to tell her that dinner was ready but found her sound asleep.

'Hey sleepy head, dinners ready. All that fresh air must have zonked you out.'

Alice sat up slowly, still feeling a little woozy.

'God yeah, I felt so knackered when we got back. It was fun though wasn't it to see it at last?'

'It was, are you feeling ok Alice?' said Grace going into doctor mode.

'I just feel really tired and was breathless after the hill climb, I'm not as fit as I once was.'

'When was your last check up?'

'I haven't had one for a few months, do you think there's something wrong?'

'You really should see someone if you feel you're worse, it wouldn't hurt to get a doctor's appointment when we get back, I'm not allowed to be your doctor as we're friends but my colleagues are just as good.'

'Please don't tell Charlie, she is worried enough about tonight, I don't want to add to it.'

'Ok, just promise me that you'll make an appointment.'

'Yes doc,' laughed Alice.

The pair headed downstairs to find the table laid, candles lit and Charlie and Jen with tea towels draped over their arms, and Holly already seated smiling, her eyes sparkling.

'Welcome, let me show you to your seat, I am your server Charlie and I'm all yours this evening,' she said cheekily to Alice.

Alice took the seat that she was being offered, smiling fondly at her love.

'Er, sit where tha wants,' Jen said to Grace.

They all erupted into laughter. Jen blushed and busied herself carrying bowls of thick and creamy leek and potato soup which she served with tiny cheese scones, which was followed by a large casserole dish with chicken and roasted vegetables.

'Tuck in everyone,' said Charlie. 'We all need the energy to dance the night away.'

After dinner Charlie removed the plates and cleared her throat to gain everyone's attention.

"I'd like to say just how proud I am of you Alice, for your amazing book about Charlotte and Hester and your love for them. Your care for them is very clear and your passion for anything you get your teeth into is contagious. So I have no doubt at all that it'll be a great success. So can we all raise our glasses and make a toast To Alice,' she said raising a glass of orange juice, the others followed suit.

'To Alice, well done lovely,' said Holly looking tearful.

'I don't know what to say, thanks guys, thanks love,' she said tilting her head as Charlie leaned forward to kiss her.

'Oh bloody hell, get a room,' laughed Jen.

There were giggles around the table.

Jen brought over a bowl of summer fruits and jug of cream and some fresh bowls. There were groans.

'I haven't room for anything else, I'm stuffed, you're going to have to wheel me into the disco at this rate,' said Grace rubbing her stomach. 'Thank you that was lovely, but I think I need to go and have a bit of a lie down before we go, do you want a hand with the washing up?'

'No it's ok, you go, we'll do the dishwasher won't we Holly,' said Alice.

Holly nodded.

'Thanks, let's go get preening for tonight sis,' suggested Jen as they both went upstairs together.

An hour later Grace got up feeling really giddy, wondering if it was a date or not, could Helen really be interested in her or was she just being friendly? After her shower she changed into black jeans and a close-fitting red t-shirt that showed off her thin figure and toned arms. Deliberating over black or red converse she opted for the black and grabbing her phone and wallet she headed downstairs to where Holly was sat in a chair by the fire with a cup of tea.

'There's a fresh pot if you wanted to grab a cup?' said Holly who was already dressed in a white midi dress and white trainers.

'No I'm good, I feel sick with nerves.'

'You do make me laugh, most days of the week you perform life changing operations, yet here you are nervous of a date.'

'I know, barking isn't it! It would just be awkward if it all went wrong and we had to work together still wouldn't it?'

'I guess, but you aren't in the same department, how often have you seen her at work?'

'Well not often, it's mainly socially really, she's a paediatric anaesthetist and I don't work in that area. I feel like a teenager who's never been kissed, Hope she isn't bonkers! You hear such horror stories don't you about dating.'

'God I know, but I know you'll be fine, and if nothing happens romantically at least you'll have made a new friend. It'll be good, it's time Grace, you deserve to be happy. Not that you need someone to make you happy, you know what I mean.'

'I do, don't worry. I might have a cup of tea, it might steady my nerves a bit,' she said getting a mug from the cupboard and pouring some tea from the pot.

Jen came down the stairs wearing a similar outfit to Grace and she was closely followed by Alice and Charlie. Alice was wearing a purple dress with matching Doc Marten boots and Charlie was smartly turned out in her blue suit and pale blue shirt.

'We're gonna have a lot of women staring at us tonight sis,' said Jen. 'You look mega in that suit.'

Charlie was paler than normal, her hair spiked up to perfection, her nose ring and labret she'd changed to a ball fitting on both, it made her face look even more striking than usual. 'Ta sis. Look I need to say this before we go. I'm worried, I was an absolute arsehole at the disco before I got sober, I'm worried I'll get flack, so if it happens I'll leave, just ring when you want a lift back, I don't want to cause any drama.'

'It'll be ok, we're with you love, the past is just where it needs to be, in the past,' said Alice, giving her a hug. 'And if it's horrible then we'll all leave. We've all got a past but we move on from it, I'm sure that's what anyone who remembers you will have done. Just look how far you've come in the last year.'

There were murmurs of agreement from the others.

'Ok enough soppy stuff, let's get this show on the road. Let's get Grace fixed up,' said Charlie grinning.

They set off for Todmorden which took them over the moors towards Hebden Bridge and then the road followed the snaking landscape of the Calder Valley.

'We have to take a tour of Hebden tomorrow before we go back. We can't come all this way and not put our lesbian stamp on the place too,' said Holly. 'I've never been before, not sure why not.'

'Yeah, why don't we find somewhere to have breakfast before we go back? Have a bit of a walk along the canal?' said Charlie, 'Look at the barges?'

'Sounds like a plan love,' said Alice looking at the shops in Hebden Bridge as they drove through it.

A short while later they pulled into the car park of the cricket club which was already filling up. Parking next to a motorhome called Edie, they headed into the Todmorden Women's Disco. They all paid their entrance fee and entered a dark room that was already buzzing with women chattering and some were already up and dancing, the red, orange and yellow lights danced around the room.

Grace scanned the room of dancing women and those that were seated but couldn't see Helen, her heart dropped, maybe she'd changed her mind after all.

Jen saw Grace looking anxious and crestfallen, so linking her arm through hers and then through Holly's she directed them to the bar.

Charlie looked anxious too. So far she hadn't seen anyone she knew, it had been over a year since she'd been so maybe her friends were right, people would have moved on. Alice took her hand and they found a table in a corner.

'It's ok love, but if you feel too bad we can always go, I just don't want you to feel pressured.'

Charlie smiled, she knew how lucky she was having Alice in her life, she was so calm and reassuring, she just hoped that she was right. It had been a big risk coming back to the place where she'd caused so much trouble, the number of women she'd had sex with after being there and then dumping them straight after, she'd honestly lost count. It was a part of her life that she really wasn't proud of. But how do you apologise to that many people when you couldn't remember their names, or what they looked like even.

Jen, Holly and Grace returned carrying drinks, all non-alcoholic beers in bottles.

'You didn't have to all not drink,' said Charlie taking a bottle.

'Solidarity sis,' said Jen taking a bottle and clinking hers against Charlie's.

Charlie smiled and looked away, her eyes beginning to water a little.

Alice took her hand and gave it a squeeze. 'It's ok love.'

They all clinked bottles together and were laughing when someone approached the table.

'Have I missed a toast?' asked the woman.

'Helen, how lovely you made it,' gushed Grace. 'Everyone, this is Helen from work.'

There were multiple hellos and welcomes and 'take a seat' and they all scooted round so that Helen could sit next to Grace.

'Glad you could make it, these are my friends Jen and Holly, and Alice and Charlie.' The foursome raised hands to welcome her.

'It's a busy one tonight isn't it; would you like to dance Grace?'

'I'd love to,' she replied and they headed to the dance floor where the Communards, *'Don't Leave Me This Way'* was playing.

They all watched as they danced in rhythm together. Helen noticeably took every opportunity to touch Grace's arm at first before taking her by the waist and drawing her in closer.

'Well she definitely likes her,' said Holly observing.

'Yeah, Fingers crossed eh, she deserves to find someone nice,' said Jen.

Everyone looked at Jen.

'What?'

'Are you turning all slushy on us Jen?' said Alice.

'Maybe,' she said snuggling into Holly's neck.

'Get a room sis,' laughed Charlie in payback for the many times she'd said it to her and Alice.

The table erupted in laughter just as the dancing pair returned.

'That was fun, I forgot how much I like dancing,' said Grace beaming.

'I need a drink, want to come help me?' Helen asked Grace. 'Can I get anyone anything?'

There were murmurs of no as they held up their almost full beers and the pair headed off.

Alice frowned and shivered.

'Are you ok love,' asked Charlie.

'Just felt like someone walked over my grave.' she said hugging her arms.

Charlie took off her jacket and wrapped it around her shoulders. 'That better?'

'Always, thanks darling.' As Charlie wrapped her arm around her and pulled her in close.

Watching some of the women dancing, and then looking over as inconspicuously as possible to where Grace and Helen were stood across the room, the gang soaked up the atmosphere and Charlie began to relax. After a while they realised that they weren't coming back to join them, instead they stayed chatting at the bar, then moved over to sit at a different table.

'Aw they want to be alone, it's very sweet,' said Holly taking the last sip of her beer. 'Anyone want a refill?'

'I'll come and help you,' said Jen. 'Will leave you both to snog in private.'

'Cheeky,' said Charlie giving Alice a full-on kiss.

'You make me melt Charlie Lowther,' whispered Alice into her ear.

'Right back at you, you look stunning tonight.'

'Thanks, so do you, wait til I get you back to the cottage.'

'Wow, ok that hit the target you bugger.' She said wiggling a little. 'You know how to get me going.'

'I hope I always will,' giggled Alice.

They kissed again and lingered in a long hug until Jen and Holly returned with the drinks.

The music changed from something no one recognised and was replaced with Soft Cell's Tainted Love.

Holly lit up, 'I love this one, come and dance with me Alice? Jen has two left feet she says.'

'Do you mind?' she asked Charlie.

Charlie shook her head, 'Go for it love.'

So Alice and Holly, followed by Grace and Helen headed for the dancefloor which was filling up with similar aged women all singing and dancing to the beat, Marc Almond's voice leading them all, everyone knew the words as they sang at the top of their voices.

Looking over at their table she saw Charlie watching her and smiling, Alice blushed. The dancefloor was really filled up to capacity blocking their view of each other for a while, the four of them dancing in pairs. Then the dancers parted and she saw Jen standing up in front of Charlie, appearing to hold back a woman with long blonde-hair who was attempting to push past her. Alice attempted to break through the crowd, trying hard to get to them to find out what was going on, but she was stalled by the dancing happy women.

Holly however was on it, she got her elbows out and parted the crowds. She had the added advantage of being tall, people moved out of the way for you.

By the time they got to the table they could hear the woman shrieking at the top of her voice. Charlie was stood behind Jen trying to make herself heard.

'You bitch, how dare you come back, how the fuck dare you. How many women here have you fucked Charlie? Which one of these are you screwing over now?' she demanded looking at the group behind her.

'Just back the fuck off, we're all here to have a nice time, there's no need......' Jen attempted to speak.

'She's got some face to come back, how the fuck dare you. You broke my heart, you led me on, and I'm not the only one, we have a group Whattsapp of the women you've fucked over.'

'Look I'm sorry, I wasn't in my right mind, I had a drinking problem, I had issues and I'm sorry I hurt you, or anyone for that matter. There's nothing I can do or say I know; just know I am genuinely sorry.'

'Are you fuck, you're all words Charlie, you always were, full of the charm, then fuck us over. I wish I'd never met you, wait until the others get here.'

'Look I'll leave, I don't want to cause anymore drama.' Charlie said, walking around Jen and attempted to get to Alice to leave.

The woman stepped in her way, standing up to her.

'You always were a coward and a user. I hate you, get your fucking arse out of here, I hope I never have to see you again.'

'You and me both,' said Charlie taking Alice's hand and walked out of the building, Jen, Holly and Grace following behind.

Once they reached her jeep she took a deep breath, there were tears in her eyes. Alice wrapped her arms around her and held her tight, Charlie burst into tears.

'Let's get back to the cottage, we can talk then,' said Grace. 'I'll just say bye to Helen.'

'No you stay Grace, I don't want to spoil everyone's night,' said Charlie. 'We can come and pick you up later.'

'Are you sure?'

'Totally, go and enjoy, be happy.'

Holly hugged Grace saying her goodbye's before they all got into the jeep and headed back to the cottage. None of them had words, silence was all they had.

When they arrived back at the cottage everyone was subdued. Alice made four mugs of hot chocolate and they all sat around in the living room.

'Anything I can do sis? Sorry you went through that, we shouldn't have gone, what a bitch' said Jen.

'I know I'm so sorry I suggested it, I just hadn't been before,' apologized Alice.

'Look it's ok, it had to be done, I wasn't going to not go and hide, but I didn't think anyone would be that bad over it still. The really bad thing is I have no idea who she is. How awful is that. Maybe I need to do something as an apology, but I don't know what?'

'You know you're sorry, and the fact that she wouldn't accept it, that is on her not you. You tried to explain,' said Holly in full GP mode.

'I guess, I'm just sorry that you all got dragged into it, do you think Grace will be ok?' asked Charlie.

Alice got out her phone from her pocket. 'She's texted to say Helen will drop her back in the morning before 9, I didn't think she'd want to go back with her tonight?'

'Me neither, love really is in the air for her,' smiled Jen.

'Just doesn't seem like something she'd do. Anyone else feel it's odd or is it just me?' asked Alice.

'No think it's just you love; we did that too though remember,' smiled Charlie, giving her a hug.

'Well...... er yes.....well,' stuttered Alice.

'We won't tell, our little secret,' winked Jen.

Alice blushed and yawned.

'Right you get off to bed,' Charlie said standing up and offering a hand to Alice, as Holly and Jen put their cups in the sink and headed for the stairs. 'I'm just going to jump onto an AA meeting, they're every hour and there's one starting in 5. Do you mind?'

'Not at all, see you upstairs, love you,' she said kissing her before heading upstairs.

'Night all.'

Charlie turned everything off and locked the door. It'd been a rough night.

She logged into the AA website and joined the international site which ran 24/7. Since covid it had been a brilliant resource for so many of the people she'd met since she became sober. Part way into the meeting when she felt comfortable with the group and the leader she shared what had happened, and how it made her feel, then she sat and listened to others. Some were at the start of their journey and others were years in. It was comforting to know she could find support wherever she was. Thankfully with her twice weekly meetings in York she'd found some peace in handling her addiction, she knew it was a lifelong battle, and there would be trials. This evening had been a definite trial, coming face to face with her past.

After the meeting was finished she did her final check around and went to bed. Alice was sleeping soundly with gentle soft snores, her blonde hair spread over the pillow. Charlie looked at her whilst she undressed, she felt very lucky and more contented than she had done in years. She just wanted to get back home, to their quiet life and the stability of York.

Chapter Nine – Pinging all the way home

After a restless night Charlie and Alice were the first two downstairs and they made a start on breakfast.

Charlie put the kettle on.

'Look, I've been thinking. I'm really not sure it's a good idea to go to Hebden today, what if we see that woman again, or someone else and there's another scene?'

'Oh love, have you been awake worrying?'

'Yeah a bit, I just don't want to spoil your trip more than it has already.'

'You haven't spoilt anything.'

'Do you think they'll be mad if I suggest we don't go to Hebden? I just can't face having another scene.'

'Sweetheart, I'm sure they'll all understand, I'm so sorry, I didn't think it would be that bad after all this time,' said Alice.

Charlie hugged her, 'Please stop apologising, it's ok I promise.'

There came the sounds of footsteps and the creaking of the stairs as Jen and Holly came down with their bags.

'Is it morning? I'm getting too old for late nights,' moaned Jen stretching.

'Sorry did you have a bad night too? I feel awful for bringing the night to a close so early and for all the drama.'

'Hey, it's on her, not you sis. Don't fret.'

'We've been chatting, is it ok if we go straight home rather than doing Hebden? Just in case,' asked Alice buttering some toast and putting it into the rack.

'Yeah, we were going to suggest that too. Anything from madam romance?' asked Jen.

'She hasn't texted since last night saying she'd be back by 9,' said Alice bringing over the teapot.

'Is toast and yoghurt ok for everyone? Sorry we ran out of bacon Jen,' said Charlie smiling.

'Just toast for me, none of that newfangled healthy stuff, is that bloody granola?' she said pointing to a bag on the side next to the yoghurt pot.

'Yup, got to look after the body,' said Charlie patting her very flat stomach.

'Nah, I'm growing old disgracefully, anyway Holly likes my love handles,' she said giving Holly a brief hug before taking a slice of toast and munching loudly on it.

There was a knock at the door.

'Ah the wanderer returns,' said Alice going to the door.

Grace came in, grinning like a Cheshire cat, Helen less so walked in behind her. 'Hey,' she said waving awkwardly. 'Just dropping and going, will ring you later Gracie.'

Grace visibly blushed scarlet.

'Ok, drive safe,' she said moving to give Helen a kiss goodbye but she was already out of the door.

'Er…….she has to get back before 11, sorry she's in a rush.'

'That's ok, now come tell us all about your night,' said Holly pulling out a chair. 'We're going to bypass Hebden if that's ok, so we're having breakfast here,'

'What can I get you?' asked Alice.

'It's ok I ate at Helen's cottage,'

'I bet you……' said Jen, who was cut off by an elbow in the ribs from Holly.

'Bloody hell Jen!' said Grace blushing again.

Alice poured out 5 cups of tea and Charlie finished off the toast and brought over bowls and spoons for those who wanted fruit and yogurt. None of them could make eye contact for fear of giggling.

'So did you have a good evening?' asked Holly.

'It was lovely, she was lovely. Very romantic,' just then her phone pinged and she jumped. 'Oh it's Helen saying thank you for a lovely night.'

'Aw that's very cute,' said Holly. 'Glad you had a good night, so definitely a date then?'

'I think so, she did say she wasn't ready for a relationship though,'

'Huh? But you stayed the night?' said Jen.

'Yeah and there was a lot of kissing and affection, maybe she just needs time to relax into it, she's only recently got out of a relationship.'

'Maybe, but be careful, we don't want you getting hurt,' said Charlie gently.

'I will. Maybe it will be nice to be casual?' suggested Grace sipping on her tea.

'Have you ever done casual?' asked Charlie.

'No, but that seems to be the norm these days in lesbian land.'

'Just take it steady, but glad you had a nice night. Right I'm going up to pack and check I haven't left anything, shall I do yours love?' asked Charlie.

'No I'll come and help. Glad you had fun sweetie,' said Alice following Charlie upstairs.

Once they got into their bedroom Charlie closed the door.

'I'm not sure about Helen, I've got a bad feeling,' said Alice.

Charlie nodded. 'Yeah, there's something off. Can't put my finger on what it is but there's something. Sorry to bring this up, but it's kind of what I did. I don't want her getting hurt.'

'I know, why get mushy with her if she doesn't want a relationship. Maybe she was just being cautious.'

'Yes maybe,' replied Charlie packing the last of her clothes as Alice zipped up her holdall.

There was a knock at the door.

'Come in,' said Alice.

Grace came in carrying her bag. 'Think I've got everything, need a hand with anything?'

'No all good here, I'll carry these down,' said Charlie taking both bags and heading downstairs.

'I'll just have one last check round, last time I left my toiletry bag and had to get the hotel to post it to me,' Alice said, having one last check around. 'Yes that's everything.'

'Are you feeling ok today, no more breathlessness or tiredness?'

'No more than normal, I'm fine honestly. Are you ok?'

Grace paused. 'I am and I aren't. I've got butterflies, and I'm never sure if that is a good or a bad thing.'

'I know what you mean, but let's think it's a good thing shall we, have you arranged to see each other again?'

Grace headed for the door along with Alice. 'Yes think we are going out in the week; she's going to ring me later.'

'Sounds lovely, let us know how it goes won't you?'

'Of course I will, thanks Alice.'

'Anytime. Right we're ready, anything need doing?' asked Alice as they entered the kitchen.

Jen was filling the dishwasher and the sides were all cleaned, it was hard to tell they'd been there.

'All done, just the car to load.'

Ping Ping.

Grace took her phone from her pocket and smiled; she started typing.

'Ooo she's keen,' said Jen picking up two bags and heading out the door.

Grace replied quickly and picked up more bags of unused food and her holdall.

Charlie was directing the Tetris organisation in the boot with the assistance of Jen when there was another *Ping Ping*.

Grace took her phone out and smiled again, quickly replying. 'Sorry guys, here's my bag, will just go help close up the house.'

'She is very eager isn't she, is that a good or a bad thing?' asked Jen.

'Not sure to be honest. Bit keen for someone who doesn't want a relationship, maybe it's just something she says?'

'Maybe.'

Alice locked the front door. 'Let's get this show on the road.'

Getting into their respective cars they set off for home.

Ping Pinging all the way.

Chapter Ten – Crisis in Stonegate

Coming home from a break away, even if it was just for the weekend is always hard. The relaxation replaced by the stresses of returning to daily life again can wipe out those gorgeous feelings and the lovely memories made within a fraction of a second. As soon as they arrived home after dropping off Grace, They were met by Di who was also the manager of Valentine's, the bar that Charlie owned and had attempted to turn into a LGBT venue. They could see her as they drove up the road pacing up and down outside the house, her face set with a worried expression.

'What's up?' asked Charlie anxiously getting out of the car.

'Don't get angry, but there's been a flood at the bar,' said Di, her face white as a sheet. 'Plumber said t'upstairs pipes been leaking, then it burst and flooded t'bar and brought down part of t'ceiling.'

'What the actual fuck Di. What's the insurance said?' asked Charlie unloading their bags and putting them on the pavement.

'Not called em yet couldn't find t' paperwork.'

'That's your job Di, to keep track of the paperwork, you did renew the insurance didn't you? For fuck sake please tell me you did.'

'Fink so, it was on't list.'

'Jesus. Can we get in the office?'

'Yeah, it's just the bar that's fucked.'

Charlie sighed. 'And you've turned the water off?'

'I'm not a total fucking nob head, of course I have. Plumber said it's been a slow leak in't bathroom upstairs. I don't know where anything is, I did look for the insurance stuff, thought it might be in your house.'

'No it's all at the office.' Turning to Alice she said, 'Sorry I've gotta go and sort this out, do you want to come?'

Alice shook her head, she still felt uncomfortable going to Valentine's which is where she found Charlie having sex with the pubs evening entertainer the previous year. A day that still haunted her.

'No I'll unpack and do some prep for work I think. Text me?'

Charlie kissed her. 'Of course love, sorry to go straight into work mode, love you.'

'Love you too,' said Alice taking hers and Charlie's bags into her house.

After unpacking and putting the washing on, Alice opened her laptop to check her emails and found one from her publisher about her book launch at the Chapter And Verse Bookshop in two months' time. Her stomach flipped, how had this happened?

It had all started with finding the hidden love letters of a lesbian couple under the floorboards of her run-down house. The women, Charlotte and Hester had both lived in her house, in a relationship that started in the 1920's. Alice as an archaeologist and historian was fascinated, so she began to look into their lives, which then had turned into a brilliant research project. At first it was something she did for herself, to see the history of her house, but after encouragement and much cajoling she sent it off to a publisher who turned it into a book. Then much to her surprise it seemed that this was something that people really wanted to read. It felt totally mad. A lot of the time she had crippling imposter syndrome, never believing she was good enough. She wished she had Charlie's confidence to deal with things.

She waded through her emails. Thankfully there was nothing too pressing as it was the summer holidays now, and only her Masters students were still working on their dissertations.

Her phone pinged.

'Hey love, I'm going to be about an hour, the place is a shit tip. Found insurance stuff and the assessor is coming tomorrow. Helping Di pack as she's gonna stay at mine, so can I stay at yours? xx'

Alice replied, *'Of course, see you soon xx'*

Taking Charlie's keys from the hook in the kitchen she went next door and made sure the spare bedroom was all set for Di and that there was some milk in the fridge. She loved Charlie's house and her taste; she was an amazing designer. They'd talked about selling both houses and getting somewhere together but Alice was wary, she'd only just rebuilt her life after her divorce from Sally, she worried so much of losing everything again. Plus Charlie had far more assets than her, she didn't want her to think she was a gold digger.

It'd been such a lovely summer, they'd had lots of time together and over the last year found they gelled so well, they could sit in silence and it would feel so comfortable, without the need to fill in the gaps of conversation. It was bliss. Far more than she'd ever dreamed it would be like. Living with Sally was frantic and she was always on edge, not feeling she was up to the mark of the wife that she wanted.

After Charlie had proposed last year they'd talked of potential wedding ideas, but they'd decided to wait until they reached their two-year anniversary before taking the plunge, mainly to keep their friends happy, but over the past few months they wondered if they could wait that long. Jen had been upset when they got together, and although things were far easier now, they didn't want to rush it. It was so hard though with the lesbian urge to merge.

Heading back to her house next door she saw Charlie walking down the street carrying a bag and a big bunch of flowers.

'For you love, congratulations again on your book,' she said handing the flowers to Alice. 'So proud of you.'

'Thanks, you really didn't have to,' said Alice taking the flowers as they both went into the house. 'Where's Di? How bad was it?'

'It's a bloody mess, can't clear up til the assessor has been tomorrow, the waters off but half the ceiling has come down nearest the front window. I couldn't find the paperwork nor the login for it at first, we're covered thank god, sometimes she's really on it, other times it's like she's on another planet entirely.'

Charlie emptied the bag on the kitchen side, some chicken breasts, assorted veg and some stock cubes.

'I've invited Di round for tea, she's packing some stuff to bring with her, she wouldn't let me help, think she might have some sexy gadgetry she didn't want me to see,' smiled Charlie.

'You'll get it back looking brilliant again in no time, I'm totally sure of that love,' said Alice. Putting her arms around Charlie from behind as she prepped the veg. 'Look what you did at Villa Roma, you turned that around totally.'

Charlie put down the knife and turned round.

'Do you never doubt me Alice?'

'Not when it comes to you and business, you've got a knack,' she said kissing her softly, running her tongue around Charlie's lips and pushing her hips into hers.

'Now that' just naughty, teasing me like that.'

'Moi, I'm good as gold.'

'Doing that you're not, bloody hell woman,' responded Charlie pulling Alice closer as she pretended to wriggle away. 'Where do you think you're going?'

'Nowhere mistress,' replied Alice coyly, biting her lower lip knowing what effect that had on Charlie.

'Fuck, I want you right now, we'll have to be really quick though before Di comes,' she said sliding her hand up Alice's leg, pulling up the dress fabric until she found her hand on the warm flesh on her thigh.

'I want to come for you, I want you to make me.'

'Shit woman, you drive me fucking wild,' she said kissing her neck, sucking and kissing in turn which turned to a very light bite.

'Harder, do it harder.'

Charlie obliged, biting her neck and lightly sucking, whilst her hand held steady at the top of Alice's thigh. Alice wriggled so that Charlie's hand shifted onto her pants.

'Naughty, but ever so nice,' as she slipped her fingers under the fabric, slipping so easily onto the delicious warm lips, then spreading them a little she slid her fingers into her.

Alice gasped and tightened around them; Charlie groaned. She was so carried away she didn't realise that her trousers had been unfastened and Alice was returning the favour.

'Oh god,' gasped Charlie. 'You bad, bad woman.'

'You're so hot Charlie,' she said pulling her trousers down a little and in a flash her hand was in the heaven of soft silky wetness. 'Fuck.'

Charlie and Alice moved in perfect rhythm, kissing and fucking, their gasps and groans echoing around the kitchen. Charlie let out a sudden cry, grasping Alice's waist as she came, her knees shuddering, her back arched, Alice could hold out no longer and exploded, her head burrowed into Charlie's chest, her legs trembling as her body shuddered, wave after wave, they rode together in the kitchen.

Slowly they stopped, enjoying the last trembles and quakes. Both of them stood in silence wrapped in each other.

Charlie lifted Alice's head up by putting her fingers under her chin, then tucked a strand of hair behind her ear, 'You're so beautiful Alice, I'm so glad you moved in next door.'

Gazing into Charlie's eyes Alice smiled. 'Me too. It's been an amazing year with you, I love you so much you know.'

'I know darling, I love you too, I'm going to spend the rest of my life making sure you know it.'

Ping Pong, Ping Pong

'Shit, that's Di, nearly caught in the act' she said pulling up her trousers and fastening them. Alice dived into the downstairs loo to sort herself out, as Charlie, a big smile on her face quickly washed her hands and headed for the door.

'Hey, come on in, will get you the keys for mine if you want to settle in, come round for dinner about 7?'

'Grand. Ok if me girl comes too?'

'Knew there was something you hadn't told me. Details later?'

'Maybe, maybe not,' Di said smiling taking the keys. 'In a bit.' And off she went over the wall.

Charlie went back into the kitchen. 'She's coming for dinner with her new bird. Ok if I carry on prepping, unless you wanted to?'

'No I'll go do some notes if that's ok that just came to me.'

'No love you just came for me.'

Alice gave a coy smile.

'You go do some writing, I can tell you've something whizzing around your beautiful brain, enjoy love,' said Charlie kissing

Alice on the forehead and headed for the kitchen where she busied herself for an hour cooking and setting the table.

She'd just about finished prepping when Di messaged to ask if it was still ok to bring her 'friend' with her for dinner so she replied *'OK'*.

Almost on the dot of 7pm Di arrived with her 'date'. They both went to the door.

'Come in. Introductions?' said Charlie taking Di's jacket.

'Lyds, Charlie and Alice,' Di said wafting her hand towards a woman obviously a lot younger than her and clearly already pretty merry.

'Pleased to meet you, come through, can I get you a drink?'

'Got any JD,' asked Lyds.

'Sorry no?'

'Vodka? Gin?'

'Sorry no, Di? I'm guessing you didn't tell her?'

'Only met last night mate, soz.'

'Ok well I'll leave you to sort that out,' said Charlie gesturing them into the living room. 'I'll finish off in the kitchen, give me a hand love?'

Alice nodded and followed Charlie through to the kitchen.

'You ok, darling?' asked Alice.

'God, thought Di would have more sense and tact and told her I don't drink and we don't have it in the house.' Charlie had been so well since being in rehab the year before. 'How old do you think she is?'

'Late 20's maybe, age is just a number though. Shall we postpone, I'm sure we could just send them next door with a doggie bag.'

'Could we? Sighed Charlie, then taking a deep breath. 'No we can't, it'll be ok. Maybe make a big pot of coffee?'

'Will do,' said Alice putting on the kettle and getting out the cafetiere.

Charlie carried the roast tin through and put it onto the dining table then added the potatoes to the mix.

'Dinners ready, come through,' said Charlie to Di and Lyds who were curled on the sofa.

'Ok boss.'

Taking seats in the dining room it became clear that Lyds didn't like the look of the food either. Alice brought through a tray with a cafetiere and cups and placed it on the table. Lyds looked unhappy.

'Got any coke?' asked Lyds.

Charlie looked over at Di, unsure whether she meant the fizzy or illegal variety.

'We've got some lemonade?' offered Alice. 'Coffee? Tea?'

'Just council pop ta, I'll get it,' and Lyds got up and headed for the kitchen taking her glass with her.

'What the fuck Di!' whispered Charlie scowling.

'What? Isn't she cool.'

'Not really, when's her mum picking her up?'

'Funny!'

Lyds came back into the room with her glass of water and slouched down on the chair.

'Shall I be mother?' said Charlie smiling, the joke totally lost on Lyds. Di scowled.

Alice picked up her plate and handed it to Charlie which she filled with a mix from the dishes, she then did her plate and Di's, then reaching out her hand to Lyd she received a blank stare.

'Food Lyds?'

'Got any crisps?'

'Sorry no,' said Charlie looking quite cross now.

Lyds got out her phone. 'What's the address I'll order something for when we get back to yours Di.'

Di was oblivious to the atmosphere around her and was spearing potatoes, chicken and roast veg into her mouth, quickly clearing her plate, finally pushing her plate away across the table and sat back and rubbed her belly.

'Cheers Charlie, think we'll be off, see you tomorrow? Are we going down to Valentine's together?'

'Sure, ten o'clock?'

'Great, let's go,' said Di and she and Lyds left.

Charlie sat utterly silent; Alice could see how seething she was.

'What the actual fuck was that! What's got into her?'

'Lust clearly,' replied Alice.

'Thought she was a mate.'

'She is thinking with other parts rather than her brain. It's ok, it won't last.'

'Most likely not, but is this why the bar flooded, was she not keeping a proper eye on things? This could mean the difference with getting the insurance payout and not. For fuck sake.'

'It'll be ok love, it's a temporary blip, you know I'll help wherever I can,' Alice said standing behind Charlie and gently rubbing her shoulders.

'I know, but seriously. What is she thinking?'

Alice leaned forward and looked at Charlie, raising her eyebrows.

'Ok I get it, that was me,' she said. 'But I'm a reformed character these days.'

'Yes there's only me you are doing very very naughty things to.'

'I want you so badly, is that wrong, I can't keep my hands off you.'

'You never ever have to love. You can play with me anytime you like, in fact I feel the need for your fingers right this minute, or are you too tense?'

'I can't think of anything nicer right now, come here and kiss me.'

Charlie turned her chair round and Alice straddled her, kissing her deeply, Charlie's hands were in her hair, caressing her cheek, holding her firmly but so carefully.

'God you're something else Alice, I bloody love you.'

'And I bloody love you too.'

Chapter Eleven – Unpacked and Picked

After being dropped off by Charlie and Alice, Grace unpacked and put her phone on charge. It had run quite low on the way back texting Helen. They weren't talking about anything in particular, but it felt so nice to be in touch even though it had only been a few hours since they'd seen each other. That's the thing with lesbian romances, they go 0-90 in a day. The fact that their first date had been over 12 hours was the norm really, however in lesbian land in some cases that would have been seen as quite short.

She'd enjoyed her company and they'd messed around a bit, the kissing had been lovely and she felt her body responding but held back. She wanted to be sure that they had more than being lesbians and being in the medical profession in common before they took it any further, but she really liked her and felt it had been mutual, especially with all the messages afterwards.

On her return Grace had wanted to go and see her parents but their car wasn't there, so instead she sent a text to her neighbours.

'Hey Lou, are you both around for that chat later?'

She put her clothes into the wash and set it going when she heard her phone *ping*. Her heart jumped.

Of course, come on over, have lunch? Texted Lou.

Sending a quick text to Helen to tell her she was heading out without her almost dead phone, and one to her parents to say she was back safe, she locked up and headed next door.

Lou and Henry, her next-door neighbours, had moved to Askham Bryan and had left London after inheriting her aunt's house. They'd settled in well to country life, having animals helped with the adjustment as everyone stops to talk to you, and if you have land then most people within 5 miles will ask if you are doing livery.

Going round the back of the house she knocked on the kitchen door, receiving a 'Come in' from within.

'Hey, how was your trip?' asked Lou. 'Come have some wine, dinner won't be very long.'

'Thanks,' said Grace sitting down at the table and taking the glass of white wine that Lou handed to her. Henry was eyes deep in the Sunday crossword, making his final mark, putting down his pen with a big beaming smile.

'There's nothing quite like finishing a good crossword, sorry Grace, how's things?'

'Good and bad, that's why I'm here to talk things through with you both. It's been quite a week!' she said taking a big gulp of wine.

'We'll help if we can,' said Lou following Grace's example and taking a large sip out of her glass.

Grace started off telling them about her parents wanting to downsize and her worries about affording the house on her own, the responsibility and not wanting to let her parents down.

'It's a good option Grace, your parents don't have to move away from the village and neither do you. Your mum grew up here didn't she?' said Henry.

'Yes she did, as did I mainly. I do understand, but wouldn't it be difficult with death taxes and things when it happens? I hate talking like this. They're both fighting fit, in fact they are going abroad on an adventure in the New Year.'

'It's a tough subject, there would be death taxes whatever you decide to do with a property of its value. Do they have other assets? Asked Henry.

'Yes, dad is always investing in property and stocks and shares. I haven't a clue what they are but know they've both got a good solicitor who handles things for them.'

'Well perhaps they can be sold when the worst happens and that will pay death duties, which would solve that part, but as for the upkeep that will cost a lot, our house isn't half as big and with the rising fuel costs it's been more than we thought it would' said Lou.

'I guess, I hadn't thought of that, I can't imagine not living here anymore, it's such a calm place. Which brings me to the next dilemma,' said Grace taking another sip. 'I'm really knackered. I used to love my job, but I'm starting to dread going into work when I'm on duty.'

'That's how I was before I took early retirement,' said Henry going over to the Aga and taking out trays of vegetables and roast pork, bringing them both to the table. Lou collected three plates and cutlery and set them on the table, they worked so well as a team, it was like a well-oiled machine watching them together. Henry started to carve and distribute and then sat down.

'Bon appetite,' said Lou.

'Thanks guys, it's really kind of you, I must return the favour.' Said Grace tucking in. 'It's been so nice to get away from thinking about work, maybe I could take a sabbatical, you know, to give me some time to think about it all?'

'Is that an option? Asked Henry.

'It could, maybe, I've known colleagues do it, I'd have to give notice but it would be possible. Maybe that's all I need is a little breathing space?'

'That might be all you need to return refreshed. I did consider that, but with Lou inheriting this house the decision was made and selling our London house has given us an income whilst I decide what to do next. I'm not quite ready for my pipe and slippers just yet,' laughed Henry.

'I'm not ready either, that's the problem, I don't know what else to do,' said Grace eating a roast potato that was a little too hot for her mouth making her eyes water.

'You ok?'

'Mmmm mmm,' said Grace taking a gulp of wine. 'Just a bit hot, sorry.'

'So what did you all get up to this weekend? Did you go sightseeing?'

'Yes we stayed in Haworth and visited the Parsonage, and also Shibden Hall where they filmed Gentleman Jack.'

'Oooo I enjoyed that series. What was her name again?' asked Lou.

'Anne Lister.'

'Ah I remember now, bit of a lesbian idol?'

'Yes you could say that bit of a lesbian hot spot.'

'Was it nice round there, I've never been.'

'It was. There was loads to see and such a beautiful area. Then to top it all off on Saturday night we went to a lesbian disco. That was a lot of fun, I actually had a date with a woman called Helen, a fellow doctor actually. It was great fun.'

'Wow that's fabulous! Are you seeing her again?' asked Lou smiling.

'Yes we're going out next week sometime, I know her from work vaguely, but hoping to get to know her better,' smiled Grace.

'Sounds like it was quite a weekend! How amazing though to meet someone. What's she like?' asked Henry.

Lou and Grace looked at him. 'Are you turning into a romantic Henry?' laughed Lou.

Henry busied himself clearing the table embarrassed.

'She's lovely, she's an anaesthetist mainly in the children's operating theatres so we don't work together as such, but she understands the hours I work, so who knows what might happen. I want to take it slow though.'

'How lovely. That is wonderful news. I hope we get to meet her one day soon.'

'Slow down,' said Grace laughing. 'We've only just started seeing each other.'

'Sorry, not sorry,' said Lou pouring Grace another glass of wine. 'Let's make a toast. 'To Grace and Helen, let romance fill their lives.'

'How many of those have you had Lou?'

'Not many, well not nearly enough,' her eyes welling up. She carried some plates over to the dishwasher whilst trying to hide her upset.

'Sorry are you ok, I've been babbling my nonsense and clearly something is wrong.'

'I don't want to put a dampener on your day, you've got so much going on already,' said Lou sitting down at the table again.

'We're friends, you can tell me anything, what's wrong?'

'Ok well a couple of weeks ago I had my routine mammogram and it found a mass in my right breast. I'm going for a biopsy on Tuesday. I'm shitting myself actually.'

'Shit. I'm so sorry,' said Grace holding her friends hand across the table.

Lou's tears which she had tried so hard to hold back broke forth and pooled down her face. Henry took her other hand.

'Any family history of breast cancer?' asked Grace.

'Not that I know of, I made the mistake of googling and wish I hadn't. It's scared me even more than I was already.'

'I get that, but let's not jump to the worst-case scenario, it could be something else? Couldn't it?' Henry asked looking over at Grace for reassurance.

'Of course, it could be fatty tissue or a cyst, it doesn't mean it's cancer, but it's good you're being seen so quickly, the sooner you'll know the results.'

Lou looked Grace square in the eye. 'I don't think it's any of that, I've been feeling off it for a while, colds I can't shift and low energy like I'm fighting something off. I think it's cancer.'

'Just know that we'll all be here for you if it is, try not to stress, I know that you are, but it won't help. What time's your appointment? I could try and pop over to the breast screening department and meet you if you wanted?'

'It's at 10.30, and I really do appreciate the offer but it's ok, I just want Henry with me, sorry,' said Lou not looking at anyone now, staring down at her held hands on the table.

'No problem, I get it, but I'm close if you change your mind. Just know we're here for you. Have you told Alice?'

'No I couldn't tell her, she would worry too much and she's got her book launch coming up, it wouldn't be fair,' said Lou composing herself. 'Anyway, I don't want anyone treating me differently, I just want to keep everything normal you know.'

'I get it, I've had many patients feel the same.'

'I don't envy you, telling people bad news, how do you cope?'

'To be honest you get used to it, I know that sounds harsh. When I first went into practice it was really rough and I lost a lot of sleep worrying, but now I know that if I've done a good job then I've done the best I can for a patient.'

'I couldn't do your job,' said Henry.

'I mean, I say all that but I lost a patient last week unexpectedly and I've been thinking of her a lot. So really, it doesn't get any easier in some ways. Some patients get to you. Especially the young ones,' said Grace trying to keep herself composed. She'd thought a lot about Juliette whilst she was away despite the excitement of getting together with Helen.

'Oh god how awful, I'm guessing you can't tell us more about it?' asked Henry.

'No sadly not, I'm hoping to find out more when I go in tomorrow. Although if it was bad news I'd already know. It's just always a shock.'

'I can imagine. Are you around for a ride later do you think? Harriet said she might come down and hack out while we still have some nice weather?'

'Sorry I can't. I'll have to catch up on some emails tonight I think and prep for tomorrow, it's so hard to get back into work mode once you've had a nice time away isn't it.'

Lou and Henry concurred. 'Well if you change your mind just give me a shout and I'll bring Max in for you later.'

'Thanks Lou. Right I better be going. Keep me posted on your biopsy and you know where I am if you need me,' said Grace giving Lou a hug before heading to the door. 'Thank you so much for the food and company. See you soon.'

She headed back to her annexe and the coolness inside, unplugging her phone, and pouring a glass of orange juice from the fridge, she kicked off her shoes and headed to her office to check how things were at work.

She loved her office, it was on the north side and was therefore the coolest part of her home, which as a menopausal woman was always a treat. She knew her parents' house was the same too, so maybe swapping wasn't such a bad idea. She'd have to really think about it and do some sums. Her idea of early retirement needed some thought too. Looking at her new fully charged phone she found a stream of messages from Helen.

'Ok thanks for letting me know'

'Are you back yet?'

'Grace?'

'Did I say or do something wrong?'

Grace sat perplexed. She'd clearly said that she was going out for a bit without her phone. Weird.

Responding she said *'All's good. Just been having lunch with Lou and Henry, hope you're having a good day, it's so hard being back knowing there's work tomorrow isn't it?'*

She pressed send and set about her work emails, there weren't many but the one she was looking for regarding Juliette was there already.

Hi Grace

Just wanted to ease your mind and let you know that the postmortem results are through for Juliette Smith. Her cause of death was a brain aneurism and not connected to her stents being inserted.

I'll send through the full official paperwork to you internally but just wanted to ease your mind in the meantime.

Her mum has left her number and wondered if you could contact her when you're next in, I'll leave that for you on your desk

See you soon

Anna.

God bless her PA Anna. She was just replying when her phone pinged. It was Helen again.

'Thank heavens, I was getting worried. What are you doing tonight?'

'I'm prepping for tomorrow, what about you?'

'Fancy a Facetime later? I've just got to sort my diary for the week so thought we could get some dates planned, what do you think?'

'Sounds good to me, give me an hour and I'll be sorted, that ok?'

'Great will call you then, bye gorgeous.'

Grace smiled, it felt so nice to be wanted, it had been a long time coming, could this be it, her One?

Chapter Twelve - Redressing the Balance

Charlie was in full swing. There was nothing quite as impressive as a butch lesbian in a crisis. She'd rallied the troops, had the insurance assessment done and she'd then got a team in to clear the debris. The 1950's pipework had been replaced and the ceiling repaired and replastered.

Never one to do things by half she'd also decided a redesign was in order despite it only being done the previous year, so damaged furniture would be replaced and all soft furnishings thrown and upgraded. It would still be a month of lost earnings but she decided that she would also use the time to redesign the décor and replace the tables and chairs and upgrade from wood to plush fabrics with love seats and sofas. It would then have a softer romantic feel. She planned the reopening for the week after Alice's book signing, and she knew she had to get onto the advertising of the grand reopening as soon as possible.

Di had mucked in a bit but had disappeared for a few days presumably with Lyds when the major graft was needed. Charlie was puzzled but not surprised. She'd done this to her before but had hoped that giving her the responsibility of running Valentine's might settle her down. Sadly it didn't look like it now.

Once the front of the bar had been cleared and the building work had begun she then had to sort out the chaos in the office. Di clearly hadn't been on the ball. She hadn't been filing invoices or keeping up to date with stock. There was a glut of some lagers and very few of others, mixers for the cocktails were sparse or missing. Charlie took all the invoices she could find back home to sort out, there were no electrics so it couldn't be done at the bar.

Arriving back home she texted Alice to tell her what she was doing and seeing what she fancied for dinner. She replied with *'You.'*

Charlie smiled, replying with *'I'll come and get you at 6.'*

Alice responded with a devils face emoji.

The accounts were a shit show. Charlie was really regretting handing over responsibility of Valentine's to Di, she was already an hour into trying to sort the mess out and still had a long way to go. Plus there would be bridges to rebuild with suppliers. She found that the reasons why the stock was low due to bills being outstanding and most of the lager at the bar was out of date and would have to be thrown. There were a ton of negative reviews on Trip Advisor about the food and service, and Charlie knew that she had a long way to go to turn things around. She needed to get hold of Di but she'd stopped answering her phone and now when she rang it went straight to answerphone. She really had gone off grid this time.

Parking that problem until the following day she headed downstairs to see what there was in the fridge, which other than a very sorry looking pepper and some celery was bare. She wondered if Alice's fridge had anything in it so popping next door she knocked and let herself in.

'Hey, it's me, can I raid your fridge?'

There was no response.

'Alice?' Charlie said checking the downstairs rooms where she saw the laptop open and an empty cup by its side.

The house was silent, so heading upstairs feeling a little worried she went into Alice's cosy bedroom, and there she was naked on top of the duvet, her hair spread over the pillow, a wide grin on her face.

'Told you I wanted you, get those clothes off!' Alice said spreading her legs revealing herself to Charlie.

'Fuck woman,' responded Charlie, stripping off and getting onto the bed between Alice's legs, she looked down on her full and beautiful body. She leant forward, their breasts nipple to nipple, a shockwave pulsed through her body and she could see Alice had felt that too. Alice sat up on her elbows and reached up to kiss her, soft kisses with intermittent nibbles, her tongue slowly caressing her tongue. Charlie slid down the bed, her eyes looking up into Alice's as she flicked her tongue around her pert nipples, they were so reactive to her touch, it was such a turn on watching the pleasure both on Alice's face and from her body's movements and twitches.

Sitting back on her heels again she took Alice's hands and pulled gently.

'Kneel up in front of me darling,'

Alice obliged, 'I want you so much, please touch me,' she asked looking longingly into Charlie's smiling eyes.

'I want you to touch me too, it was so hot the other day, I want to do it again but not so rushed, I want you to really enjoy it.'

Alice began to tweak Charlie's nipple and she mirrored her, each copying the other exactly, all the time kissing and watching each other build up the tension and desire.

Alice followed Charlie's lead when she made her way slowly down over her belly and into the warmth and wetness between her legs, parting her lips and began to flick the clit back and forth making Alice jump.

'Very sensitive today darling?' she asked softly continuing to flick.

'Oh god I can't stop twitching, what are you doing?' she asked giggling.

'Teasing you, I want you to really enjoy sweetheart, take your time.'

'Oh my god. Fuck.' said Alice doing the same to Charlie whose clit she could feel had swollen so much as she flicked it softly.

'Harder,' asked Charlie.

Alice flicked a little harder, Charlie jumped.

'Harder.'

She applied more pressure and flicked faster, Charlie was reacting, arching her back as she pulled Alice closer, then curling two fingers she pushed them deep into Alice making her gasp and then let out a loud groan. Alice did the same, the reaction was mirrored as they both faced each other fingers still within each other. Their eyes magnetically sparkling, the gaze was intense.

'Now what shall I do next?' asked Charlie tilting her head and kissed Alice. 'How about this,' as she slid out her two fingers and then pushed three inside her making Alice groan even louder and the grip was so tight. She was so utterly lost in the moment that her fingers came out of Charlie and slid them up and down her soaking clit. They began to ride the fingers, both gyrating and pressing themselves into the loving fingers, kissing became frantic and the moans of joy and ecstasy were louder and louder, echoing around the silent house.

Charlie could sense how close Alice was, so manoeuvred her thumb onto her clit as she slowly slid onto her fingers, the air was charged around them and the duvet beneath them was soaked from how excited they both had become. Charlie knew it wouldn't be long so taking out her fingers she focused on giving her the utmost pleasure moving her fingers round and round and then over the top, applying pressure then lessening until she exploded, her whole body taken over by the intensity of Charlie's love, passion and desire for her. This in turn led Charlie to come too, her cries of joy as the feelings swept over her, they both rode the wave as long as they could. Locked into mutual love and desire until they both collapsed giggling onto the bed from how intense it had all become, but so amazing too.

'God, that was something else......'

'Absofuckinglutely!' exclaimed Alice.

'How long were you waiting for me?' Charlie asked quizzically.

'I heard you knock so thought I'd surprise you, don't think I've ever got undressed so fast. I've been thinking about you all day, in lots of naughty ways.'

'Have you now,' said Charlie playfully tweaking Alice's nipple making her curl up and put her hands playfully over her boobs.

'I have, you're so hot, how could I not.'

'Well I'm not sure about that, but I've been thinking about you too,' she said rolling Alice over to face her so they were lip to lip. 'I love you Alice, let's get married, or start planning it, I really want to be your wife and you to be mine. Not in a possessive, I must have you way, I just want to show you and the world how much I want to be with you and to be legally yours. To do with as you please as often and for as long as you want.'

'I love the sound of that, I love you too. Let's do it. Marry me Charlie, I want to be yours forever too. You are all I have ever wanted; you do know that don't you. I never dreamed I could feel like this, to be so desired and listened to. You just really get me, you know me, you know what I want before I know it myself. I want to feel like that, with you for as long as you want me.'

'I'll always want you. I'm not as good as you at saying how I feel, I'm not as romantic or as caring as you, but you've made me a better person, I've learnt so much from you sweetheart. You have brought me so much joy, I never thought anyone would love me. Well let's face it, I was too quick getting them out of the door for that to happen. But I knew as soon as I met you, on the doorstep of your house when you moved in, that there was something different about you. I couldn't get enough of you do you remember. I'd find any excuse to talk to you, even making an absolute tit of myself at times. You get me too. You don't judge me; you encourage me to be the best version of myself that I can. I love that about you, I really do.'

They laid and held each other, locked in a blissful cloud. Charlie stroking Alice's hair and Alice laid with her head on her chest.

'I want to run another idea by you,' said Charlie.

Alice sat up a little and looked up. 'What's that?'

'How about I sell my house and move in with you? It seems daft to have both houses now, we spend more time at yours which I love, what do you think, give it some thought I don't want a decision now, I just wanted to run it by you.'

'I've been thinking similar thoughts too, but what about if we sell both houses and buy somewhere together? I'd really like to live somewhere quieter, it's a lovely street but the York traffic does my noodle in most days. But I know you have business stuff here.'

'That's an even better idea, why didn't I think of that? I wanted to talk to you about Valentines.'

Charlie saw Alice slightly recoil.

'I'm going to sell. Di isn't interested and has quite frankly let it go to the dogs, and I've been so busy with the lakes project I haven't noticed, that's on me. I know you don't want to go there and it would be lovely if we did something together. Not sure what yet, but I want us to be together properly.'

'Really, but you love Valentine's.'

'I loved the idea of it yes, and it was a success to a point, but it was supposed to be a gay venue, but it's not that anymore, no one goes out, or if they do they aren't coming to York centre anymore. I don't blame them frankly. Who wants to walk down the street avoiding the vomit?'

'True. But are you sure? What else would you do?'

'You know me, I'll find a project. I'm seriously thinking of downsizing as I just want a quieter life with you.'

'Wow. Are you sure, I know you loved your life.'

'I did, but having to go off and leave you all the time is really getting me down. I'm not saying I want to be joined at the hip, which would drive us both bonkers. No, what I'm thinking is just do something local. Once the bar reopens I'll put it on the market I think, give it a few months to build up a good reputation again. But think I'm done with it.'

'What about the lakes? That's going well isn't it?'

'It is, and I promised the family I'd keep it going, and I will. I'm just going to take a back seat. The youngest brother has really got the love of the place and I'll help out if he needs me, but I just want life with you. I don't want to go galivanting off all the time, I want to wake up next to you every day for the rest of my days.'

Alice could see that Charlie was looking emotional but tried and failed to hide it. She snuggled into her chest.

'I want that too; you are such an incredible woman. Let's do all of it. I love you sweetheart.' Said Alice. 'So when are we going to look on Rightmove?'

'I thought you'd never ask, pass me my phone,' said Charlie laughing.

Chapter Thirteen – Hope and all its friends

Returning to work Grace threw herself into her emails and missed calls, including the one left for her by Juliette's mother. She initially got no reply so left a message on the voicemail, but after a morning of missed calls they finally got to speak.

'I hope you don't' mind me contacting you,' asked Juliette's mum. 'I wondered if I could ask a couple of questions.'

''I'll help where I can yes, what is it you want to know?'

'Did you see her when she came in with her heart attack?'

'No sorry I didn't, I only saw her on the ward when she was waiting for her stent fitting, why?'

'I don't know if she came in alone or with anyone, is there a way of finding out?'

'I could have a look to see who her attending was in A&E and then see if they remember if there was anyone.'

'That would be helpful thanks, I hate to think of her going through all that alone.'

'I know that once she was on the ward after her admission she didn't have any visitors, I asked her and she said no one was coming, I know she made a call after we talked and one before she died as the ward staff told me, but I don't know to whom she spoke sorry. Do you have her phone?'

'Yes I got it with her belongings, there are a ton of messages but I haven't read them yet, think they're from her girlfriend, or ex. God she was a piece of work, hope she doesn't come to the funeral.'

'I am so sorry for your loss; I'll be in touch as soon as I have any information for you. It might take a while though with holidays and shift patterns.'

'That's fine, I just need to know.'

They said their goodbye's and Grace brought up Juliette's notes on the screen from when she was admitted to A&E and she sent emails to the doctor on call and also a couple of the nursing staff to see if they remembered anything. She wasn't expecting anything to be honest, it was a fraught place to work and remembering visitors who came in with patients wasn't high on their priorities. But it was worth a try.

Later Grace had got home from work whilst there was still enough heat and light to tidy up her small garden around the annexe. It was equally relaxing and frustrating. She'd had such plans for it, roses around the door, some deep borders with hydrangeas and fuchsia bushes and a nice patio area, but of course work always got in the way, or she was too knackered when she got home to worry about it. Today however the goddesses aligned and she had time and the energy to do a bit. It also gave her the ideal placement to see when Lou and Henry got home from the hospital appointment.

Lou had texted earlier to say that the biopsy appointment had gone well and Henry had taken them both out for the day to take their minds off what happens next. That would be one of the worst things, the waiting on the results.

Around 7, just as it was starting to get dark, Henry's black Freelander drove slowly passed Grace's annexe on the lane they shared and pulled into their parking area behind the house. So, putting down her gardening tools she headed out of her gate to greet them.

Lou got out of the car gingerly.

'Need a hand,' said Grace going to the passenger door side.

'No, it's ok, just a bit sore now the painkillers are wearing off.'

'Do you want to come over for a drink or do you just need to settle?'

'Thanks for the offer but I just want to lie on the sofa with a bag of crisps and a gin and tonic and watch something crap on telly. Come and join us if you like?'

'Ok, I'll just go freshen up and be over in 5. Get the gin out Henry!'

So after a quick change and a thorough hand wash Grace headed next door with a large bouquet of flowers and a card that she and all their friends had signed.

Going round to the back door she called out 'Hello,' and went into the kitchen as the door was open. Henry was arranging another bouquet of flowers in a vase as Lou looked on from the kitchen table, dabbing her eyes with a tissue.

'They're from Alice and Charlie and were on the doorstep, so sweet of them to remember.'

'Here's some more from me and a card from us all, how are you doing?'

'Thank you, you didn't have to, everyone has been so kind,' said Lou dabbing her eyes again.

'Bless you, it's ok. Was it awful?'

'It was worse than I thought, painful, not how the leaflets and the internet said. More like it was happening to someone else and went on for longer than I thought it would. It's very sore.'

'How long before you get the results?'

'They said a couple of weeks, but who knows, it's going to be hard waiting. Any tips on how to take my mind off it?'

'How about going away for a few days? I could sort the horses if you wanted, might do you good to not be sat around waiting?'

'We talked about that on the way home, I think we might, that's if you don't mind looking after the house and the horses.

We might go down to Cornwall and see some of Henry's family, walk on the beach and forget for a bit. What do you think?'

'That sounds totally perfect. Saves stressing about organising flights and things, roads will be busy though.'

'Henry suggested we set off in the middle of the night to avoid that, take it in turns to drive.'

'Sounds a good plan, just send me a message if you decide to go and what needs doing.'

'Of course, let me get you the spare key for the back door and the alarm code in case we do, always handy for you to have them,' said Lou going over to one of the kitchen drawers, retrieving a key and writing down the code on a post it note.

She handed them over to Grace. 'It'll be ok won't it,' she said seriously.

'I truly hope so Lou. I better get going and finish off the garden, let me know if you decide to go.'

'Will do. Thanks for everything,' she said giving Grace a hug as she left. Henry did the same and walked out down the path with her.

'She's putting on a brave face but she's really scared.'

'She's bound to be, it's massive, but I do think going away for a rest and some peace would be a good idea. I'll hold the fort whilst you're away.'

'Cheers Grace. Take care and we'll message if there's news.'

'Just go and relax, you might have a rough time ahead, just take the time for each other. See you soon.'

Grace waved goodbye and returning to her garden she picked out some weeds in the path and border. Sitting back on her heels she smiled as her phone pinged and seeing it was a message from Helen her smile spread wider across her face. They'd been messaging a lot since the mini break and they'd shared their shift patterns and aligned a date the following evening. The plan was for dinner and a movie, then maybe she could be dessert thought Grace. She didn't want to rush things, but on the other hand it was exciting to share stories and the flirting was exhilarating. It had been some time since anyone had shown any interest that went beyond fumbling and disappointing endings.

After seeing what Lou was going through the feeling of life being too short struck deep but also not doing the full lesbian U-Haul in the blink of an eye. But yes she had to hope that this time things might just be different. Just this once.

Chapter Fourteen – What Dreams are Made Of

Grace needn't have worried. The first month had been bliss, being treated to meals, weekends away when they could fit it in with their work schedules, and best of all round the clock sex. Grace had never felt so wanted.

The sex had been something else, the passion between them, they couldn't keep their hands off each other, within minutes of being in the same room they were undressing each other in haste, belts ripped off and buttons sometimes being dislodged and flying across the room. It was bliss, and for the first time in years she'd felt herself relax into feeling safe and content.

Helen wasn't always forthcoming with arranging dates as time went on. She was elusive at times. Didn't respond to messages and the late night Facetimes stopped. But in every other way things were great and Grace felt happy and began to relax into what she felt was a grown up relationship. She didn't do any actual planning but the dreams she had in her head were of a future with Helen that was long lasting.

However this unexpectedly changed. They'd been sat watching a home buy and selling programme on the sofa, marvelling at multi-million-pound houses when Grace got overly comfortable.

'Wouldn't it be amazing to live in one of those houses on the beach, with a balcony and those incredible kitchens. Imagine the breakfasts looking at the sea,' said Grace dreamily.'

'Who with?' asked Helen, pulling back from where they had been snuggled under the blanket.

'Well you of course.' replied Grace, her head still in fantasy land.

'That's a bit much. We aren't anywhere near that,'

'Sorry I was just…….'

'You know I'm not ready to play happy families, I don't know if I ever will.'

'Sorry, I was just in fantasy land, I didn't mean to make you uncomfortable, I'm happy with how we are now,' said Grace, hoping Helen wouldn't know she was lying.

'Are you?' she said standing up abruptly, Grace momentarily falling over on the sofa after Helen moved. 'We aren't even in a relationship!'

Grace frowned thinking *'we aren't?'*

But rather than say anything she said, 'You know I was only thinking out loud, it wasn't meant seriously, we aren't anywhere near that.'

'No we aren't. And if you carry on like that we won't ever be.' Helen went to the island and picked up her keys. 'Think I should go, it's all a bit much.'

Grace stood up and followed Helen to the door.

'Please don't go, we can't leave it like this.'

'You are just too full on, I need space, you know that.'

Grace knew nothing of the sort, this had never happened before. Helen had intimated thoughts of the future with her before, retire to somewhere near the coast, have a happy life with her, grow old together, tonight she'd just been following the lead from previous conversations. Now she was in the wrong.

Helen walked out; her foot fall audible as she speed walked over the gravel to her car. The roar of her engine to emphasise that she was angry. Grace worried that it would have alarmed her parents and neighbours.

Sitting back on the sofa, picking up the discarded blanket off the floor Grace burst into tears. What should she do?

Her initial thought was to call Lou but pride stopped her, she was going through enough as it was. No, Grace couldn't involve her in what was going on with what was a new 'relationship' or whatever it was.

She felt stupid. She'd been gushing about how fabulous Helen was to everyone she knew; she was so proud to think she was her girlfriend. Tonight however it appeared she was being placed firmly in the friend zone and maybe only just friends with benefits, a place where she never wanted to be. She'd genuinely thought this was a relationship, it certainly felt like it some of the time, all the phone calls, texting, spending all their free time together. Nighttime talks when neither of them could sleep. What else was that but a relationship, or the beginnings of one. Certainly not a sex as and when Helen felt like coming over situation.

Picking up her phone she dialled Helen who would be home by now. It rang twice but it went to voicemail. Helen had declined her. What the hell?

Cleaning up their glasses and bowls of nibbles she headed to bed, the bed that still smelt of their love making, well without the love part it appeared.

Lying in a ball, hugging her knees she eventually cried herself to sleep. The clock on the wall ticking away the time she didn't seem to have with Helen anymore.

The following morning she woke to the sound of her phone pinging with a message from Helen.

'Morning sweetheart. How did you sleep?'

Grace shot up in bed grabbing her phone staring at it. After last night how could she message her with that kind of message. How could you treat somebody like that and then expect them to be happy with a good morning sweetheart message?

Grace replied, 'What was last night about? I don't understand how everything seems fine for you this morning, after all you said last night.'

A few minutes later Helen responded with 'It was nothing sweetie just letting off steam. I've been under such pressure lately; you understand don't you? My job is so pressurised, the long hours, having to deal with staff who don't listen. It all got on top of me.'

Grace felt paralysed to answer, worried she would poke the bear and start everything off all over again. So for a quiet peaceful life she kept quiet. The way she had for most of her life where relationships were concerned.

'OK, is there anything I can do to help?'

'Can I come over?'

'Of course I'll put the kettle on.'

'No need, we won't be using the kitchen,' laughed Helen. 'But you could warm the bed up for me.'

She was in two minds of what to do. Part of her wanted to say no, don't come over, but she knew they needed to sort things out. Maybe they could when she got there.

Helen arrived 20 minutes later; Grace had done as she was told and was waiting in the bed for her, leaving the door on the latch.

She heard rustling in the kitchen, of something being put on the island, and Helen unzipping her jacket. She then came into the bedroom and beckoned Grace towards her. 'Come here,' she said firmly.

Grace obeyed. Walking towards her slowly. Helen immediately pushed Grace against the wall, sliding her hands underneath her T-shirt straight to her nipples, tweaking them hard. Grace let out a loud gasp.

'Is that what you like? Tell me what you want.' Helen said forcefully.

'I want you.'

'You want me to what?'

'To do what you want with me.' Grace was putty in her hands despite the previous evenings events.

'Anything?'

'Anything,' Grace said in a whisper, her breathing deep, her eyes looking intently at Helen's. She'd never seen her so fired up before.

In the blink of an eye Helen removed Graces top throwing it across the room. Returning immediately to tweaking, pulling, then intermittently softly caressing her nipples. Grace could hardly stand upright, a combination of pain and softness and complete desire in Helen's eyes turned her on, more than she'd ever been in her whole life.

'Does that feel good?'

Grace nodded she had no words, the concentration to stay upright, her knees buckling, she could feel how aroused and wet she'd become.

Helen began moving her hand slowly down until it rested at the top of her pubic hair. Grace gasped.

'Is that what you want? Tell me what you want.'

'I want you; I want you to fuck me. Please.'

'Please? Say it again.'

'Please Helen, please fuck me!!'

'I wonder if you're wet enough for me. I'll be cross if you aren't, maybe I won't fuck you.'

'Please,' Grace pleaded. 'Oh god, please.'

Helen slid her fingers down and parted Grace's lips, she was so wet.

'Nice and wet, just as I wanted.' Helen began kissing her breasts, moving slowly down her stomach then went down on both knees.

'Put your leg over my shoulder; I want to look at you.'

Grace lifted her leg and rested it onto Helens shoulder, trying really hard not to topple over. She could feel Helen's breath on her and hear her quietly groan.

The anticipation waiting for Helens next move made the moment even more erotically charged. She could sense her mouth getting closer to her, the softness of her breath, listening to the gentle moans that they were both making.

'Do you want me? Do you want me to fuck you?'

'Yes,' gasped Grace. 'Yes more than ever. Please!' She begged.

Helen moved her right hand under Grace's leg and lifted it up higher, exposing her even more. Helen moaned loudly.

'I'm going to make you come so hard. Do you want that?'

Grace had no words now; she was all jelly and mush and desperate to be touched. She managed a rough, stilted 'Yes'.

Helen leant hard into Grace's clit, her tongue flicking hard, then pulling back so it was just the tip, then repeating, then suddenly she pulled back.

'I need to see you more,' she said moving Grace's leg back to the floor. Then standing back up she took her by the wrist and pulled her to the bed, pushing her down, then using both hands pulled the top of both legs until they were in the air, parting them as wide as she could.

She'd never felt so hot, desired and close to coming without really being touched.

'Beautiful, you desperate?'

'Yes,' nodded Grace, equally wanting this to last but also wanting to come right there and then.

Kneeling between her raised legs Helen parted her lips again, totally exposed she slipped in so many fingers she could feel herself being stretched, it was equally good and bad but being so wet her fingers moved in and out perfectly.

Grace gripped the duvet, her body moving up and down the bed with the force of Helen's fingers and just when she thought she would explode, she stopped and bent down and began sucking her clit hard. That was the final part, Grace couldn't take anymore and she came, crying out loudly.

Helen didn't stop as Grace rode wave after wave of bliss. Then she began fingering her again, softer and slower, feeling her fingers curving inside her, it felt so good as the waves built up again, gripping and desperate, she moved with each stroke, until they were both in unison, gasping. Grace partially sat up resting on her elbows. Helen began kissing up her belly, passed her breasts and up her neck eventually kissing her, mouth covering hers. This tipped Grace over the edge again as she fell back onto the bed, her back arched as she came. Helen climbed onto the bed and laid on her back next to her, Grace rolled over and snuggled up to her, her fingers beginning to undo the buttons on Helen's shirt.

Helen stopped her. 'It's ok, I'm good, I got off on watching you come.'

'I really want to touch you,' said Grace, still aroused and desperate to give her so much pleasure as a reward.'

Helen sat up, doing up the buttons then she stood up and went out of the room.

Grace sat up, stunned. She could hear cupboard doors opening and the kettle simmering, the oven door opening. So putting on her dressing gown she went out into the kitchen.

'Are you coming back to bed? I could make breakfast if you wanted.

'You go back to bed. Chop chop, get the bed warm.'

Grace did as she was told and returned to the bedroom, puzzled.

A short while later Helen came into the bedroom carrying mugs of tea in one hand and a plate with some croissants on.

'Where did they come from?' asked Grace.

'I know how to treat a woman. Brought them with me, freshly baked this morning at the Blue Bird Bakery.'

Helen handed the plate to Grace and put the mugs on the bedside table, then stripping off she got into bed. Taking a croissant she tore a piece off and fed it seductively to Grace, teasing her lips with it before she let her take it. She ripped off another piece and repeated the process, taking a small bite herself, then fed the rest to Grace.

'I brought another present with me, want to see?'

Grace nodded, her mouth full of delicious croissant.

Helen went back into the kitchen and came back with a red present bag with rope handles.

'Close your eyes,' she said.

Grace closed her eyes; she felt the plate being taken from her.

'I want you to lie down, open your legs.'

Grace giggled but did as she was told, but held the duvet under her chin, slightly apprehensive.

She felt Helen move across the bed and inbetween her legs. Then she heard the buzzing, she gasped.

'What .... Oh my god'

Helen had really shocked her, what was she going to do? The anticipation made her feel breathless, she could feel it vibrating against her knee as Helen slowly traced it up her leg, and when she got to the top she moved it back down her other leg then back up again, moving it around her pubic hair, then down gradually, the pulses were just delicious, sending shockwaves through her whole body.

Helen moved it lower; it was gliding easily as she was so wet from what Helen had done to her before, now she was repeating it, she'd never felt so desired. So wanted.

'I want you to kneel up for me,'

She felt Helens hand in hers, pulling her up until she was knelt up on the bed.

'Spread your legs,' she commanded.

Grace obeyed, she could feel the vibrations on the bed but then felt it trace up her leg, onto her clit and then she almost toppled over as it was thrust into her, holding it still she felt the pulses rippling through her, she wanted to stop, but she also wanted more, it was too big, but it felt so good. She'd never really used dildo's or vibrators before, god she felt she'd seriously missed out.

Helen moved it slowly in and out, her groans matched Grace's as her legs began to start shaking as the rush of feelings swept over her, their mutual gasps were loud, neither couldn't contain themselves much longer. Then a new sensation took over Grace and suddenly she felt a rush of liquid running down her legs and onto the bedding. Her whole body began to quake. Her knees giving way as Helen removed the vibrator and switched it off. She sat back on her heels amidst the very large damp patch on the bed.

'What was that? I feel so embarrassed,'

'Don't be, you just came, that was so very hot, I really want to taste you, but I don't think you want to be touched again?'

'As hot as that sounds, I don't think I can take anymore,' replied Grace, she felt like she was floating out of her body, with a mixture of warmth and cold sensations through her. She slowly laid down on the bed and Helen laid by her side.

'I want to make love to you too,' she said turning to face her. Reaching out her hand and touching Helen's face, pulling her in closer to kiss her. She pulled back.

'It's ok, I just can't be touched, I came when you did, I am perfectly satisfied watching you.'

'Are you sure? I really want to kiss you, show you how much I loved that ……………………love you.' Said Grace softly.

Helen looked back at her like she'd been shot, her eyes wide open. Staring.

'What?' said Helen sitting upright and standing up. 'How can you be in love with me?'

'Sorry, it slipped out, I do though, I didn't mean to make you feel uncomfortable.'

'This is too much, we aren't in a relationship, I told you I didn't want to be in one. Then this?'

Helen grabbed her clothes and headed into the living room, Grace hurriedly put on her dressing gown and went to find Helen, who by this point was almost fully clothed and was pulling on her boots.

'Please don't go, we need to talk about this, I didn't mean to make you feel uncomfortable. Helen please stay.'

But Helen was no longer listening, she took her keys off the kitchen table and walked out of the door yet again.

Grace burst into tears, sitting down on the kitchen chair sobbing in total disbelief. Abandoned again.

Chapter Fifteen – The Signing

The day of the book signing had arrived, Alice woke with her stomach in knots. The bookshop had said for her to get there for around 1pm and looking at the clock it was only 5.30. She felt exhausted. Charlie had got in late after another day at Valentine's prepping it for the launch the following week and she was totally exhausted too. Di still hadn't reappeared so she was on her own with it pretty much, her sister Jen helped out where she could and Alice too, although she still hated going there.

Attempting to get up quietly she'd just swung her legs over the side of the bed to sit up when she felt Charlie's arm wrap around her waist.

'Where do you think you're going darling,' said Charlie pulling her back under the cotton sheet which was all they could bear being on them due to hot flushes. Menopause was the gift that kept on giving.

'I was just going to check everything was ready,' said Alice snuggling into Charlie.

'You checked it about fifty times last night before bed, you're all ready. We just have to turn up and you'll sit there pretty and welcome your audience.'

'But what if no one comes? What if it's a flop,' said Alice quietly.

'They'll come, your publishers have put it out there, it will all be fine I promise. You get to talk about Charlotte and Hester and it will be amazing.'

'Hope you're right.'

'Want some tea? Toast?'

'I couldn't eat a thing, but tea would be lovely thanks, I'll make it as I was almost up.'

'Nope, you stay where you are, this is your day and I'm taking control today.'

'I like the sound of that,' said Alice smiling, raising both eyebrows suggestively.

'Cheeky. You're a bad influence, let me go make some tea, are you sure that's all you want?'

'For now yes please love,'

Charlie put on her pyjamas and headed downstairs. Alice lay back on the pillow looking up at the ceiling. In the night she'd had every scenario going through her head, no one arrived for the signing, or people came and heckled, complained about the price and the million pens that wouldn't work when she tried to sign the books however many she tried. She took a deep breath, she knew it would be ok, Charlie and her friends would be there too and if no one came they'd all come back here and commiserate with pizza.

Coming back into the bedroom Charlie handed Alice a mug of tea which read, Worlds Greatest Author on it.

'Aw that's so sweet thank you,' she cried, putting it down on the bedside cabinet and hugging Charlie who had laid down next to her.

Taking an envelope out of her pocket of her dressing gown, she handed it over to Alice.

Opening it she read:-

May all your dreams and wishes come true today

You deserve only the best in life from all the goodness that you put out into the world.

We're all here to support you today as always.

Have the best day authoress

All our love Charlie, Jen and Holly xxxx

'That's so beautiful of you all, I don't know what to say.'

'You don't need to say anything, just enjoy your day. Now drink your tea, there's more I want to show you.'

Alice picked up her cup as Charlie went out of the bedroom and she heard her go out of the front door, returning a few minutes later popping her head around the bedroom door.

'Delivery for Alice,' she said producing a huge bunch of flowers and a smart red present bag with gold rope handles and put them on the bed. 'The flowers are from me and the bag is from Jen and Holly. Lou and Henry are bringing theirs later.'

'I don't know what to say, thank you darling.'

Alice smelt the flowers, beautiful pale pink roses, such delicate petals and so fragrant. She smiled putting them down on the bed and opened the bag. Inside was a card and long blue box with gold lettering. Opening it up gently she found a pink fountain pen with a gold nib.

'Oh my god I've always wanted one of these, it's so beautiful, did you tell them?'

'I did, they asked what you'd like so I suggested the pen, I've seen you drooling over their adverts.'

'That's so thoughtful, thank you for telling them, I'll text them, now where's my phone?' as she began searching her bedside cabinet but returned empty handed frowning.

'Can't you find it?' said Charlie smiling.

'Ok what have you done with it?' Alice said grinning from ear to ear.

'I'll have to ring it to find it then won't I, maybe you should dial?' she said handing her phone to Alice.

Alice tried to find her name amongst Charlie's contacts but couldn't find it.

'I can't find my name,' said Alice puzzled.

'Have a look for Future Wife.'

Alice scrolled down and saw Future Wife and her phone number.

'That's so beautiful darling thank you,' said Alice welling up. 'Shall I press ring?'

Charlie nodded.

Pressing call there was a pause and then her ring tone coming from the wardrobe, so standing up she headed over to it and opened the door, following the sound of the theme tune to The Detectorists which was her favourite programme on television. In the bottom of the wardrobe was another large gift bag with a wrapped box in it.

Taking the bag over to the bed she took it out and stared down at the box wrapped in beautiful wrapping paper.

'It looks too good to unwrap, did you wrap it?'

'No, it'd look like a car hit it if I'd done it, come on open it up, I'm dying to see your face.'

Alice began to slowly, and carefully unwrap the present. Once all the paper was removed it revealed a turquoise box which when she opened it there was a beautiful Italian brown leather laptop bag come briefcase.

'Oh heavens Charlie. It's amazing, it must have cost you a small fortune!' exclaimed Alice.

'I wanted my authoress to have the best for her big day. Even if you just put your sandwiches in it. Well done darling.'

Alice hugged her, 'I don't deserve all this.'

'You do, and one day I hope you'll realise just how special you are, not just to me but to your friends too.' Said Charlie kissing her on the forehead. 'Are you feeling nervous?'

'Very. How long before everyone arrives?'

'We've hours yet, what would you like to do? I know something that would take your mind off it.'

'I'm sure you do but I don't think I could relax, is that ok?'

'Of course, what about a walk by the river? It's a lovely day outside, the sun has come out especially for you. You might feel like breakfast after?'

'Sounds a good plan, let me throw some clothes on and we can get some fresh air.'

'Is there anything you need to take with you?' said Charlie putting on some jogging bottoms and a T-shirt.'

'Nothing, the books are already in the shop, we just have to turn up just before so they can set me up. God I hope people come!'

'Come on, let's get some air,' said Charlie ushering her down the stairs and out of the house.

Charlie was right, the late autumn sunshine and the river were an amazing combination at that time of day, when a lot of York was still asleep and it was peaceful. The ducks were still huddled on the riverbank as two crews of rowers went past at super-fast speed, breaking the stillness of the River Ouse as they went past, creating a wake that lapped the shore disturbing the ducks in turn.

They walked the circuit up the riverbank coming out at Lendal Bridge, taking the stairs up to walk the route home on the path that went past 2 St Leonards Place, the house that had featured so heavily in Charlotte and Hesters love story and the place where Alice had collapsed outside the previous year. It was like coming full circle.

The city was beginning to wake up, cars were queuing at traffic lights and impatient cyclists bypassed the red lights to get to their journeys faster. Drivers shook their heads at the interlopers, equally in disgust and envy of their breaking the law.

Returning home Alice went upstairs to get showered. Charlie needing a distraction heated up some croissants and laying the dining table with jams and marmalades and glasses of orange juice.

Coming downstairs Alice stood in the dining room doorway and sighed. 'You spoil me, thank you,' taking a seat as Charlie took the other. She felt so moved at all the effort Charlie had made for her.

After they'd finished eating Alice cleared the table and went to get dressed whilst Charlie went to have a shower. She double checked her email on her phone which was inside the sparkly new briefcase and sent a text to thank Jen and Holly who replied with *'On our way!'*

'Jen and Holly are on their way,' said Alice as Charlie came back into the bedroom with a towel wrapped around her. Her tattoos on her arms speckled with droplets which made the patterns come alive somehow.

'Great, let's get this show on the road,' she said getting a shirt and trousers out of the wardrobe. Most of her clothes were at Alice's now which felt weirdly comforting. For such a long time she had felt like this was her home more than the house next door.

Alice put on a new pale blue linen suit which contrasted with Charlie's dark blue and they headed downstairs just as the doorbell rang announcing the arrival of Jen and Holly, closely followed by Lou and Henry.

'I thought you were both meeting us there later,' asked Alice beaming.

'Lou was too excited to wait so we came early,' said Henry. 'How are you feeling?'

'A bit nervous, but excited now too. Thank you both for coming.'

'We wouldn't have missed it for the world darling. I can't wait to read your book, and here's a little gift to help with whatever you write next, we hope you like it,' said Lou handing another giftbag, this time this one was gold with hearts on it.

Alice took it into the living room and sat on the chair to open it. Inside was a red box with tissue paper inner, and upon unwrapping it she found a black leather journal with an organiser and calendar inside.

'Oh, it's so beautiful, I don't know what to say, thank you so much,' said Alice clutching it to her chest.

'We all put our heads together and got you some things we knew you'd love, but would also be practical too,' said Holly. 'Have an amazing day, how exciting.'

'Why are you all here so early, we don't have to be there until 12.30?'

'We're taking you to the Grand for brunch as a special treat.'

The Grand was a decadent five-star hotel in York City Centre, a place she had always wanted to visit, especially to eat there.

'Oh wow, thank you all. I feel utterly spoilt; this is the best day ever.'

Jen came into the living room eating a bowl of cornflakes.

'What have I missed?' she said spooning in another mouthful.

Anyone else would have asked Jen what she was doing eating before they went out for brunch, but Jen was a force of nature and was forever hungry.

'I was just saying thank you to you all, for everything. I'm really touched.'

'It's nowt, you deserve it. What time's brunch?'

'We've got to be there for 11, Charlie has booked us a private room,' said Holly.

'Fab, knows how to treat a lass does my sister,' replied Jen turning to take her bowl to the kitchen.

'Right let's get this show on the road,' said Charlie. 'Let the lady of the hour lead the way,' she said gesturing for Alice to go first.

The gang headed out to The Grand, the streets of York were buzzing with tourists and traffic, people all heading to places with anxious faces, except for their group who chattered and laughed all the way there.

The staff showed them into an elegant Edwardian room with a table laid out for eight where they were all treated to a spectacular brunch with everyone but Alice tucking into the spectacular feast.

'Sorry I can't eat much, my stomach is just churning with nerves,' said Alice.

'Don't worry, I just wanted you to start off the day with something to distract you. You look so beautiful today,' said Charlie leaning over and giving her a kiss.

'Get a room,' said Jen smiling.

'We've just booked Henry's 60th birthday party here, well one of them,' said Lou. 'He's decided to end the year with a bang so be prepared for a month of invites. Might be worth not eating between now and then too.'

Everyone laughed, Henry was renowned for his entertaining and over feeding.

The waiters came in carrying trays of cakes with Grace behind them.

'So sorry I'm late, the traffic was horrendous,' said Grace, who looked fraught and tired.

'Don't worry, there's plenty left, help yourself,' said Holly. 'Did you have a late shift; you look ever so tired.'

'No, I've had a couple of days off, I'm just not sleeping well,' said Grace. 'Are you excited about today Alice?' Grace sat down at the far end of the table. 'Oh god, I've left your card and present in the car, I'll go and get it,' she said standing up.

'I'll come too, I could do with a breath of fresh air to stop the butterflies,' said Alice following Grace out of the polished large wooden door.

Outside in the car park, the sun shone down on the tarmac, in the light Grace looked even worse.

'Are you ok? You look so tired,' said Alice.

'All's good. Just busy, life, universe and everything.'

'How's Helen? Are you managing to see each other?'

Grace began shuffling and looking down at her feet, not making eye contact which wasn't like her, her normal bubbly and happy countenance had faded.

'It's just been a rough week; work has been super busy as a colleague is off sick and Helen ....'

'And Helen?'

'Erm, I don't know, she seemed so keen but I've not heard from her in a couple of days. We keep having silly squabbles. I think I'm too much for her. I've messaged, but nothing back, she was supposed to be coming with me today.'

'I'm so sorry, but well that's bloody rude, everyone has a minute to send a reply. And no you're not too much!'

'I know I keep telling myself that, but my head has been making excuses up that maybe something has happened, maybe she just changed her mind.'

'But even so, surely it's common courtesy to send a message or ring? I don't get it.'

'Maybe she is just another ghoster, got what she wanted and off they go. She's been acting really weird, and has said some awful things.'

'Really? That's not on at all. I'm sorry Grace,' said Alice stroking Grace's back.

Tears appeared in Grace's eye and she wiped them away subtly hoping that Alice wouldn't notice.

She had.

'Come here,' said Alice opening her arms to hug Grace. Grace sobbed on her shoulder. 'It's ok, I'm sure there will be some kind of explanation, just you see. But she really shouldn't be saying bad things to you. Do you want to tell me about it?'

'Maybe, but not today,' said Grace pulling back, retrieved a tissue from her pocket and wiped her face dry. 'I think I'm just tired and hormonal. Don't know why it's got to me so much.'

'Because you're like me, a romantic, you want to see the best in everyone. It'll be ok, just a blip maybe?'

'Maybe. God why does life have to be so hard, I thought that we were good. Guess I was wrong.'

'Give it time, it's early days, I know you already sort of knew her but you don't really get to know someone properly for ages. You do need to sleep though, how are you coping with work?'

'I'm not really, I'm just doing clinics for a while, I asked my boss for a break when my colleagues come back, that'll help. I guess I just want a piece of what you and Charlie have, you just seem so happy.'

'We are most of the time but we have our ups and downs, but thankfully less downs these days, it takes time. Come here,' said Alice opening her arms so she could hug Grace again. 'Let's go back in and have another cup of coffee and get this show on the road.'

'Let me just grab your present,' said Grace heading to her MG parked outside. She returned a few minutes later with a neatly wrapped parcel.

Alice unwrapped it to reveal an illustrated edition of Jane Eyre.

Alice opened the book and looked inside. 'Oh my god, this is stunning, thank you Grace,' she said hugging her. 'It's beautiful, did you get it when we were away?'

'No I sent away for it; I know you've probably read it a million times but wanted you to have this special version.'

'I feel so spoiled by you all, thank you.'

Together they walked back into The Grand and into their dining room and were just sitting down when the door burst open and Helen came in, her face red and her eyes transfixed on Alice, not Grace.

'Helen, what's wrong?' said Grace standing up and walking towards her. However Helen really wasn't happy, her face and body language totally shut down and clearly angry blatantly ignoring Grace as she spoke and walked towards her. 'Can I get you some tea?'

'What's going on with you two then? I saw you both out there, you looked over friendly, don't you think you ought to be honest with me?' Helen said, welded to the spot and glaring the whole time at Alice.

'What do you mean? We were outside talking. I don't.......' said Grace.

'Don't give me that crap, I fucking knew there was something going on, with your weird arse friendships,' Helen raged.

'Weird? I don't...'

'For god's sake, be honest, you're fucking Alice on the side, why show interest in me and do that. And you Miss Fuck around sat there thinking you're something, when your Mrs is messing you around, it's a joke. You're all a joke,' she said pointing at Charlie.

'Now look here, I don't know who you think you are, just shut it.' Said Henry standing up, his napkin falling onto the floor. 'You're talking total nonsense.'

'I don't understand?' Charlie took Alice's hand which was shaking under the table. 'Helen, you've got this very wrong, there's nothing between them. What gave you that idea?'

'Come on, admit it, you were out there hugging and laughing, looked pretty intimate to me.'

'Then you were very much mistaken,. We're just friends,' retorted Grace. 'Please Helen, don't spoil Alice's day.'

'Isn't everyday Princess Alice's day? Look at her, sweetness and light, butter wouldn't melt, guessing going out with a cheating partner, it's rubbed off on you,' said Helen smirking.

'Now look here, just get out, enough now. Go and fuck right off,' said Lou walking round the table and adopting a sheltering stance in front of Alice.

The whole table turned and stared at Lou, it was very rare of her to swear or lose her temper. Henry was gobsmacked, his mouth open.

'God, you're all the same aren't you, bloody incestuous. Don't bother contacting me again, I don't want any part of this circus.' Helen turned and left the room leaving the door wide open. Grace who had panic in her eyes ran after her.

'What the actual fuck? Who the hell does she think she is, think we should go after them?' said Jen.

'I'll go, you need to get to the book shop, I'll catch you up,' said Henry leaving the room.

'Are you ok? What was that about?' asked Charlie.

'No idea, I gave Grace a hug outside as she was upset. You don't think I ……'

'God no! Just didn't know why her head went there.'

'She's clearly bonkers,' said Lou.

'Clearly. When did a hug ever mean something more? I don't understand her, but then again I don't want to understand. Come on, I'll go sort the bill and we need to shift it or we'll be late. Sure you're ok?' said Charlie.

'Don't worry I'm good, I just hope Grace is ok.'

'She will be fine, Henry will sort it, just give me 5 and we can get off.'

True to her word she returned a few minutes later and they all headed out to the Chapter and Verse bookshop.

They were greeted by the shop manager, a jovial young woman, her hair tied into a rough bun at the base of her neck which looked like it was threatening to escape.

'Lovely to meet you Alice, we've set out a table and your books over here,' she said leading the way. On the table, which was on a raised platform, nestled into the History section, on which lay a pile of Alice's books, a bottle of water and a pen. 'We've had a lot of interest in your book signing today, will you be saying a few words before you start?'

'I hadn't thought of that. People are actually interested?'

'Yes, we've had emails and I know a few arrived early and have gone to the coffee shop upstairs.'

'Wow. I had no idea.'

'Now is there anything else I can get you or your friends?' she asked turning to look at the Charlie and her friends.

They all shook their heads.

'Ok, well I will come over at 1 and introduce you, relax. This is your day; you'll be absolutely fine.' She said walking back towards the till area.

'Oh my word, I honestly didn't think anyone would come!' Alice exclaimed.

'Of course they will, we are so proud of you darling,' said Charlie pulling out the chair for Alice to sit.

Alice sat and made herself comfortable, taking out the fountain pen her friends had bought her. Looking up she saw all her friends forming a line in front of the table, Charlie at the front.

'What are you doing?'

'We want to be the first to buy your book. We're your biggest fans after all,' she said beaming.

'You really don't ....'

'We want to, now can you make mine out however you want.'

So Alice took up her pen and wrote a message to Charlie.

To my darling Charlie.

Thank you for all your love, care and encouragement,

I love you more than words can say.

Forever Yours.

Alice xxxx

Alice blew on the ink to dry it, turning it for Charlie to read.

'Gorgeous, thanks darling,' she said leaning over the table for a kiss.

'Get a room,' said Jen playfully nudging Charlie out of the way. 'Reet, make mine out however you like, none of that slushy stuff mind.'

Alice smiled, then taking out her pen she wrote:-

To one of my oldest and dearest friends Jen, thank you for being your bonkers self, don't ever change. Thank you for being there at the beginning of all this. Alice xx

Alice again blew on the ink and turned the book around.

'Sorted. Grand,' said Jen taking the book and pretending to be deeply engrossed in it so as to not draw attention to the tears pricking her eyes.

Then one by one all her friends had a book signed and they all headed to the till to pay for them. The shop manager returned at a few minutes to one as people came down the staircase and others walked across the shop floor to the table and formed a crowd of around 30 people. Alice recognised some as work colleagues but the majority were strangers.

The manager cleared her throat.

'Afternoon all, thank you for coming today to the book signing of Alice Hargreaves and her book Charlotte and Me, over to you Alice.'

Alice took a deep breath and stood up.

'Thank you for your introduction,' she said smiling at the manager. 'and thank you all for coming,' turning to her audience. 'The book was a labour of love, brought about when I bought my lovely house and found a box of love letters under the floorboards. Finding out more about the women who wrote them, discovering the love story between them and where they lived was both beautiful and heartbreaking. The book gives both a biography of both women and their story, but also the history of lesbians from the 1920s onwards, the houses they lived in and places that they visited. I hope that you all enjoy it. Thank you.

Alice sat down and a round of applause began, started of course by Charlie and her friends, but followed by the rest of the audience.

Once the noise subsided Alice, blushing, sat down and her first purchasers approached the table to get a signed copy. At the beginning the queue was to the door of the shop and slowly but steadily got longer until they were out on the pavement, but by the end of the two hours the queue had dwindled down to four young women, tattooed and pierced quite openly flirting with Alice who was totally oblivious. The shop workers quietly topping the pile of books up next to her as it rapidly lowered.

After their copies had been signed and paid for the manager made her way over back to the table where Alice was packing up to leave, chatting with her friends, beaming from ear to ear.

'Well that exceeded more than we expected, well done Alice, you've sold 84 copies. That's amazing for a debut writer. Well done. I look forward to reading it if you wouldn't mind signing one for me too?'

'Of course, I'm so sorry I've forgotten your name, it's been quite a day.'

'Totally understandable, can you make it to Ella please.'

'Of course.' Alice signed the book, twisting her right wrist around, 'God it aches now,' she said grimacing.

'Not surprised at all. None of us are used to writing anymore are we. That's a very pretty pen by the way.'

'Thanks, it was a gift for my book signing,' Alice said gesturing towards her beaming friends, who were also now joined by Henry and Grace.

'Thanks for signing this for me, I'll leave you to your friends. Well done again.' Said Ella heading back to the tills.

'Sorry we missed the main event; how did it go?' asked Grace walking up to the table. 'Is it too late to get a book?'

'Of course not, but are you ok? Did you sort things out?'

'Is it ok if we don't talk about it now,' Grace said grimacing. 'It's your day and I've already spoilt some of it.'

'You haven't spoilt anything at all, don't be daft,' said Alice taking the last of the books on the table, signing it and handing it over to her.

'Thanks, I'll give it a read this week. How brilliant you're a published author. You're incredible you know.'

Alice never one for receiving compliments played with the lid on her new pen, then put it safely in the inner pocket of her jacket. 'Shall we head out now? I'm gasping for a cup of tea.'

'Your wish is my command,' said Charlie taking Alice's hand as they headed out of the bookshop waving goodbye to Ella and the other staff. 'I've booked us for afternoon tea at Betty's in the Belmont Room.'

'You're kidding me? I've wanted to go there forever, oh my god thank you, what did I do to deserve you?'

'I told you, it's your special day, enjoy every moment of it my love.'

'I absolutely am, thank you, are we all going?'

'Of course, daft head, we don't want to miss a minute of it either,' replied Holly. 'Plus it's a new food experience for Jen.'

'Grub is grub,' she said smiling. 'Hurry up gassing, I'm starving.'

Chapter Sixteen - Reopenings

Having worked like a trojan for weeks, it was finally time for Valentine's to reopen at the end of November. The renovations had taken a lot longer than expected, Di had disappeared and was totally off radar, so Charlie had to advertise for, and appoint a new bar manager Luke, and she planned to put the business on the market as a going concern in the next few months. Her staff of course were disappointed but she'd assured them she would see them right.

Alice had offered to help out but she knew she found it hard to be there, too many bad memories, which was another reason that the business had to go. She knew it was prime real estate so would sell quickly despite the slightly depressed market, but it would clear her to build new plans for the future with the woman she loved. Charlie had never felt so happy.

It wasn't the sort of happiness you get with the hormones flying and love you's in the air that don't mean a thing, it was the feeling of total contentment and excitement of what the future might hold for them. They had so many plans, fantasy ones like selling up and moving to the Maldives, and reality too, Charlie had her house valued and it was going on the market the following week. Once she made a decision, her head was 100% focused on it. Alice was ecstatic and she was positively glowing.

Charlie unlocked the door; the lights were already on inside and she saw Luke behind the highly polished bar stocking up the bottled beer and generally being the organised man he had shown himself to be at interview.

'Hey, how're you getting on? Need a hand?'

'Nah, all in hand boss. We've been in an hour making final checks, these beers came in just now from the local brewery so we're all set. The pianist is just changing and the bar staff are having a quick break. Did you want to go over the menu?'

'I'll have a look but the floors all yours Luke, I'm just here for a bit in case you need a hand, you never know how many will turn up at these things, especially with it being the Christmas Market today too. Could be a busy one.'

Luke handed Charlie a paper menu, it was as well laid out and presented as any she had produced herself in the past. She smiled at Luke.

'Cheers, this looks incredible. I'll just go through and see the chef, see if they need a hand.'

Luke smiled, he'd heard of Charlie's work ethic, which was one of the reasons he'd taken on the role. He was sad though she wanted out of the business.

After checking the kitchen Charlie went and sat in her office, well Luke's office now. It was on days like this that it all felt worthwhile, though she knew this was the last one. She logged onto her Google drive and opened up a business plan she had been working on for a while.

In her head it had all started when she'd proposed to Alice. She'd not said anything but she'd been Googling hotels and venues of where they could hold their special day. There were so many to choose from, but none grabbed her. She knew they could personalise everything down to the napkins and favours, but she wanted more than that for her and Alice, especially knowing that what her previous wedding to Sally had been like.

Alice had told her that it was a rush job, Sally insisting on keeping it small and private, she called it intimate but in reality it was so she didn't have to tell her colleagues at the solicitors office that she'd got married. She didn't hide her sexuality, just her relationship with Alice. It had caused so many upsets but she'd continued to do it regardless. So Charlie knew she wanted to give Alice the day of her dreams, surrounded by everyone who loved her, and all her friends from however far away they lived. There would be no expense spared too.

This is when her other idea came into her head, what if they bought somewhere and created their own wedding venue? She'd looked on the market and seen big houses for sale with land, industrial units that would make for something interesting and quirky too, but what she really loved as soon as she saw it was a farmhouse with land, and many outbuildings in the village next to where Lou and Henry lived. It came with a few large 18th century stone built barns which would be a perfect place for the wedding to take place with an adjoining old large cart shed which would be perfect for holding the reception. It had an old dairy which the current owners had already converted to use as a kitchen so food could be prepared on site too. Their accommodation would be an almost derelict farmhouse desperately in need of everything doing to it but the project didn't scare her, she just had to broach it with Alice at some point soon. Financially she knew that Alice didn't have that kind of money, but she had enough assets to cover the cost of the farm and still be able to afford the renovations.

Her head had been swimming with ideas over the past year and the figures were looking really good, so taking the bull by the horns yesterday she'd called the estate agent and made an appointment to see the newly listed farm that afternoon. She'd go herself first and take Alice the next time if it was any good. So after a couple of hours of making notes in her file, checking on the bar periodically after the doors had opened she closed everything down and said goodbye to Luke and the staff. The bar was half full after only an hour of reopening, always a good sign of things to come. Word of mouth would do the rest.

Collecting her car from the car park she made her way to Askham Richard on the outskirts of York. A beautiful village with a pond, quaint cottages and a large green with a pagoda in the middle. It was of course well known for housing a large womens prison in its centre, but that didn't detract from its beauty. Charlie also knew that the village held special memories for Alice too. Her grandfather had worked at the big house called Askham Grange during the war. That's where he'd met Alice's grandmother, so it always felt special when they went through it or stopped at the pond to while away a few hours watching the ducks.

The farm was just on the outskirts of the village down a short drive which was laid down with hardcore with huge potholes, but nothing her Jeep couldn't handle though. The agent was waiting for her at Ashfield Farm when she arrived, suited and booted in his finery. He was from one of the poshest agents in York, but Charlie matched his style as she was dressed similarly. She got out of the Jeep and greeted him with a firm handshake.

'Charlie Lowther?'

'Yes, thanks for coming on short notice What can you tell me about the farm?'

'It's been on and off the market for about a year on and off, but the owners are now keen to sell, you do know that there's a lot of work needing doing?,' asked the agent.

'Yes I saw from the details, I'm looking for a project.'

'It's certainly that. Do you want to start with the house or the outbuildings?'

'Outbuildings I think first, then the land?'

He nodded and led the way into what had once been a fold yard with some stables on the left and two large barns at the top and side. They were all in their original state.

She'd felt that this was the right place as soon as she turned into the drive. The farmhouse although dilapidated was pretty, not unlike Alice's old cottage in Terrington, she could picture them both there and she hadn't even stepped foot in the door.

The agent led the way to one of the barns, it had two large wooden doors held closed by a long bar, and a stream of dust could be seen through the daylight that shone down from the holes in the roof. It gave the barn an atmosphere of mystery, and it took her breath away as she looked around at its potential.

'This is one of two large barns, both structurally sound, they both need new roofs, but they have a lot of potential and there might be chance of planning for change of use. What were you thinking of doing with them? Hobby farming or holiday lets?'

'I'm thinking more of an entertainment space. Do you know of other buildings in the area that have managed to get planning around here?' said Charlie, her eyes darting around, admiring the barns original beams and the slit windows. She could picture them all dressed up with lights strung around, being hired out for weddings and parties. This could be perfect for that she thought.

'There's been a few yes for housing, and a couple of holiday lets, but you could always have a word with the planners see what they say. It's already had a change of use for the milking shed to the owners business kitchen, they make cheese there. It's really successful actually, they're moving further down south to a bigger farm, we can have a look inside in an hour when they finish work if you don't mind putting on some PPE.'

'No problem at all. What land is available? It said 5 acres but more could be available,' asked Charlie who knew nothing at all how big a 5-acre field was. They went into the second barn, it too had many holes in the roof, but its charm far outweighed the damage that could be seen.

'They are selling off 100 acres in parcels. So you could buy the whole farm for offers around £1.5 million or the farmhouse and buildings and the 5 acres for around £950,000. It depends on how much you want to deal with. The land that comes with the house wraps around the back of the buildings and house and has entrances from the lane, handy if you wanted to create new access.'

'That's good then. I've never dealt with land before, how much land would I need say for a horse? Can you keep one on its own?'

The agent smiled. He began to think Charlie was a time waster. 'Thinking of getting a horse?'

'My girlfriend loves horses and if we buy something with land it'd be lovely for her to have one of her own again.'

'Well you need 1.5 acres per horse roughly but they do need company, you don't fancy getting one for yourself? If so 5 acres would be sufficient.'

'Nah, not for me the horses. I prefer two feet on the ground at all times. Dangerous buggers horses. Can we go into the house now maybe? I want to see if its habitable or if we'd have to stay elsewhere whilst its renovated.'

'It needs a new roof and fully modernising, some of the ceilings upstairs are down so I'd say no to living in it, unless you like a lot of dust in your cornflakes,' he said laughing.

'I've done my share of that thanks but it's not something I care to repeat.'

'Done this sort of thing before?' he asked letting them both into the back door.

'Yes I've been renovating bars and restaurants for years, done a fair few flats and houses too. Time to settle down now though, start a new life and business too. I've been liquidating my assets so I can do something fresh.'

The agent suddenly realised he had a genuinely interested client, he then turned on his full charm offensive as he showed her round the house. It was in a bad state, a bird had been nesting in the kitchen chimney and there were many feathers and droppings as they walked around the empty property. The kitchen floor was heavily cracked and had a thick beam above the large open chimney.

'There used to be a cast iron range there, ripped out years ago, perfect place for an Aga,' said the agent in passing.

Charlie again smiled inside, she could get Alice the Aga of her dreams, losing the cottage where she was married to Sally had really broken her.

'The owners don't live here then?'

'No they moved out a few years ago, they just farm here and live in a barn conversion up the road. Shame to see a house so neglected, but the right person with the right vision will put that right I'm sure,' he said looking out of the corner of his eye at Charlie who clearly was in full buyer mode. He was surprised she didn't worry about getting her suit dirty as she stuck her head into cupboards and tested out floorboards, even sticking her head into the loft where more birds had definitely been having a long party in there.

'Do you want to look at the land now, and then we can go into the dairy?'

Charlie nodded, a far off look on her face as she envisioned the things she'd like to do to the house. She'd keep all the original fireplaces and delph rack that went around most of the downstairs rooms, but the ceilings and cornicing would have to go, the ceilings looked weak and ready to come down on their own. But it wasn't anything she was worried about at all. She always liked a challenge.

The land consisted of a large grass field that wrapped around the house like the agent had described, it slopped upwards towards the back and had hedged boundaries. Charlie had no idea if this was a good thing or a bad but presumed that if it was ok for cows then it would be ok for horses too. She didn't walk far into the field, there were black and white cows grazing there, their huge udders swaying a little as they walked and grazed.

'Not really a cow person, where do they get milked if the dairy is converted?' asked Charlie.

'They get herded up the road twice a day and milked at the next farm, proper countryside traffic jam. I'm guessing you aren't from a country background.'

'No, but I think me and my partner are both ready for the quieter life. We both live near town which has its perks don't get me wrong, but the peace you would get here, cow traffic jams permitting, would be heaven I think.'

'Let's head over to the kitchen and we can have a look around there, then if you've any questions I'd be happy to answer them.'

Charlie nodded. The country air filled her nostrils and although the house and buildings were rough and ready, she saw the potential for a proper home with Alice.

The old dairy was the only building that looked perfect, it had a new roof, windows and the stone had been lovingly repointed with lime mortar. So often she'd seen them daubed in concrete and knew that a damp house or building would be found once the door was opened. If this whole farm was done up properly, well then it would preserve it too. The workers in the barn were just getting into their cars, an older woman waved at the agent as she got into her car and drove off.

'That's the owner, she said that if you wanted a second viewing she'd be happy to take you round. Answer any questions etc.'

'Great thanks,' said Charlie.

They entered the dairy through the door the workers had emerged from and went into a changing area where they donned hair nets, gloves and an apron to go over their clothes. Going through a further door Charlie found herself in a kitchen that sparkled, its stainless-steel counter tops, shelves and large fridges were just what she'd hoped to find. The rest, such as a cooker and burners could easily be added so food could be prepared. Yes, this really was the perfect place.

Exiting a short while later Charlie tried hard to hide her enthusiasm but knew in reality that boat had sailed. She'd given the boat away that she was keen.

'Thanks for showing me round, I'll be in touch about another viewing,' said Charlie shaking the agents hand.

'No problem Ms Lowther. Here's my card with the owners number on the back. If you've got any questions just call.'

Charlie nodded.

They both said their goodbyes and Charlie headed back home, her head spinning with fabulous ideas, she just had to do a bit more working out then she could see if she could get Alice on board with the plan. It would be a big ask.

Chapter Seventeen - Plans Ahoy

Life as an archaeologist wasn't at all like in the films. There was no running down tunnels being chased by boulders, nor strutting your shit in Lycra around relics and ancient buildings. Instead it was hours of trawling through mud with a brush and trowel, finding bits of pot or wall, or up to your eyeballs in old bones, putting them together like a macabre jigsaw puzzle.

Alice's life consisted of a mixture of the two, but with the added fun of sitting in the archives, giving her eye strain at old handwriting and floor plans of long forgotten industrial buildings. This is where she was heading on a chilly December morning. She'd left Charlie in bed as she didn't have any plans until late morning. She deserved a lie in after the hours she'd spent organising the reopening of Valentine's. She'd also been working on a new plan, that was the thing about Charlie, she was always full of surprises. She never sat still, Tigger like as always. She hadn't told her what the new plan was yet, but she could tell how important it was to her because of how many hours at a computer screen she was spending.

Alice's university work had been manic too. Her promotion meant a bigger workload and hours of prep at home on an evening, but she loved her job and Charlie had been so supportive of her progress. The past year had been such fun, especially with her book launch, whirlwind trips to the lakes to check on another of Charlie's projects, as well as occasionally house sitting for Lou and meals with Jen and Holly.

Alice knew how lucky she was. Besides Jen and Holly they were the only lesbian couple still together amongst their friends. Seeing and hearing about the struggles Grace was going through with Helen made her especially thankful.

However the joy of the year had been watching Charlie and Jen forge a sisterly connection. This had been slow initially but they were becoming more settled in each other's company, and she and Holly had taken a step back to allow them to bond.

The previous week had been the start of Henry's 60th birthday festivities, an event he was going all out on. So far it had involved parties, drinks and copious amounts of food. So after trying to squeeze into her jeans one morning Alice dragged Charlie out of the house for some much-needed fresh air and to hopefully burn off a few pounds before even more Christmas parties.

Now walking really wasn't Charlie's thing, in fact she did almost anything to avoid it. Her Jeep was pretty much welded to her backside so getting her out walking in the countryside had proved a challenge.

After a few grumbles they were soon driving off out into the countryside towards Harrogate and over towards the reservoir at Fewston, parking up and putting on their warm jackets, gloves and hats.

Charlie looked miserable. 'Are you sure you don't just want to go watch a film?'

'Come on, it'll be fun, just a bit of a walk and some fresh air. You're always at the laptop, it'll do us good I promise.'

They both set off at a slow pace, arms linked walking a slightly muddy path up into the trees that surrounded the reservoir, it was steep at first then a gradual decline until they came to a small track which Alice set off purposefully along.

'Do you know where you're going or something?' asked Charlie, puffing.

'No, just want to see where this goes, come on, it'll be fun.'

Charlie mumbled something inaudible under her breathe. Alice stopped and faced her, giving her a long kiss. 'That better?'

She smiled 'Give me another and I'll tell you,' she said cheekily pulling Alice in closer, sharing another deeper kiss. 'That's more like it.'

'Now that is a nice way to have a walk.' said Alice. 'Let's just go up this way a bit, see where it goes to.'

Charlie nodded. They continued walking up the track, through long grass, over rough stones then to an open clearing where a large derelict building stood, with trees and bushes growing out of where windows once were and the roof had long since caved in.

'Wow. Take a look at that!' exclaimed Charlie. 'Nice renovation project.'

Alice smiled and quickened her step, poking her head into where the doorway once was. 'Bloody hell its huge, I'll just take some photos.'

Charlie smiled.

'What?'

'I love seeing you all excited.'

'I know you do,' said Alice with a cheeky glint in her eye. 'You've got your renovation head on, I can tell.'

Charlie smiled and nodded, she hadn't broached the subject of the farm yet, she'd instructed a surveyor and a builder she'd used before to go round for quotes so she knew just what she was letting herself in for. There was no point getting Alice's hopes up if it was all going to cost too much.

Taking out her phone Alice took some external photos and some from the doorway, not daring to go further in due to the overgrown trees and plants, and the walls looked precarious. The floors above had long since fallen down and the roof had totally gone but the remnants of fireplaces could be seen in the upper walls. She looked on her phone maps which pinpointed roughly where they were so she took a screenshot for later.

'Fascinating. Wonder who lived here, it's massive?' asked Charlie.

'I'm guessing it was the housing for workers from a cotton or wool mill that was down near the river, will check when I get back, sorry Charlie, all our outings seem to end up historical.'

'It's so hot when you get all fired up about history stuff. Cleverness is very attractive you know.'

Alice blushed. 'Come on let's go back and find the car, you deserve a treat at home.' She said winking.

'We don't have to wait til we get home.'

She took hold of Alice's hand and took her into the forest, the twigs snapping under foot, the only other sound were the gentle giggles from Alice. Reaching the foot of an enormous oak Charlie took Alice in her arms, turning her until she was leant against its thick trunk.

'Is this ok?' asked Charlie 'We've never done this before'

'You know it's my fantasy'

'I do.' Said Charlie, undoing the top button of Alice's jeans which was always a turn on, as was when her two fingers undid her bra strap so fast it took her breathe away.

Alice gasped as Charlie slid her hand down her trouser and into her pants.

'Shit.' Said Alice, the urgency of Charlie wanting her was turning her on so much. The desire that she saw in her eyes was immense, her gorgeous eyes willing her on as her fingers slid gently over her clit. The intensity of the feelings, whether that was because it was risky doing it in public, or because of the desire between them both, Alice couldn't contain herself and she let out a loud groan as her knees buckled and came hard on Charlie's fingers, she leaned hard onto her, willing her to slide her fingers in.

'Please.' She begged.

Charlie obliged and Alice buckled again, kissing her hard, totally lost in the moment of the two of them so deeply in love, so full of passion. Alice loosened her grip of Charlie's back who slowly removed her hand from the wet underwear, her wet fingers tracing up her stomach and fastened her trousers for her again, patting them after she'd done so with a cheeky smile on her face.

'Now I could really get used to walking if this is what you mean.'

'Perfect way to finish I agree.'

'And finish you did,' said Charlie taking Alice's hand as they walked back to the lane and passed the ramshackle building again.

Alice suddenly tripped and looking down saw that her right bootlace had come undone and was dangling in the mud. 'Just a sec,' she said carefully walking, picking her feet apart so as not to get tangled and trip.

'You look hilarious, like you need a wee,' laughed Charlie.

'Ha ha,' said Alice approaching a pile of stones she lifted her right foot and started to tie her lace. Just as she was about to stand up something caught her eye. She bent down and traced her fingers along a large stone that had fallen down behind the others.

'You ok?'

'Yeah, come here, can you see letters on this stone?'

Charlie looked at the stone, bending down and touched it too. 'Looks like a name, can't make out what it says, can you? Shall we scrape some of the crap off?'

Alice let out a little chuckle, 'Moss Charlie, not crap,' Alice giving her a peck on the cheek then began scraping the moss away with her thumb, the letters becoming more visible, reappearing after years of being hidden. There were two lines of letters one began with E and the other with a G, and as she gently scraped along more letters appeared.

'Do you think this says Eliza?' asked Alice.

'Yeah, the other one says Gert, Gertrude?'

Alice scrapped away a little more, revealing more letters, Dagnell next to Eliza and Marr next to Gertrude. 'I'll make an archaeologist out of you yet.'

'If excavations involve woodland sex then I'm up for that!'

Alice smiled standing up, her hand in the middle of her back grimacing. 'God my back hurts, I'm getting too old for this lark.'

'I'll run you a nice hot bath when we get back home, what about the stone, whats it about?'

'I don't know. I'll have to do some research. Let me just pinpoint where we are,' Alice got out her phone and again screenshotted where they were using her map app. 'That'll do, let's head back, I need that bath and your hands in that order when we get home.'

So hand in hand they walked back to the car, a spring in both their steps.

Chapter Eighteen – Two Soups

The following day Alice and Charlie woke as normal, wrapped up in each other, the duvet on the floor, a sheet covering them. No matter what the temperature was outside they always had a large fan blowing across the room thanks to the menopause. They'd spent the night at Charlie's house as they often alternated between houses depending on who cooked that evening.

Charlie got up first, telling Alice to stay in bed and that she'd bring breakfast up, but after looking down at their bloated stomachs they both agreed to skip it and have tea instead. Lounging in bed really wasn't their thing, they were both up with the lark women and today was no exception. So Alice grabbed her pjs and dressing gown and slipper socks that Jen and Holly had bought her the previous Christmas. Charlie had matching ones, but so far had resisted putting them on.

A short while later Alice descended the stairs and hearing clattering coming from the living room went in search of what the noise was.

Charlie was on her hands and knees cleaning out the wood burner and laying a new base and getting it going again, it had been well used so far this winter and was so cosy on an evening.

'I was about to bring up your tea, guessing you've got itchy feet to do some work?' asked Charlie.

'You know me so well!'

'I knew you wouldn't be able to resist it love, I saw that spark in your eye yesterday.'

'What when you were fucking me against the tree?' asked Alice smiling coyly.

'God you get me going, you're so hot, come over here and let me kiss you.'

'Well yeah, after you've washed your hands.'

Charlie looked down at her black and ash covered hands and laughed. She beckoned Alice over.

'I wasn't planning on using my hands.' She said kissing Alice, teasing her and pulling away.

Alice sighed. 'God you are so tempting! You're a gorgeous distraction.'

'I do my best.' said Charlie kissing her softly then went off to the kitchen to clean up and to make the promised tea.

She returned a short while later with a tray with two cups of tea and some warmed croissants.

'They smell divine, aren't we supposed to be being good?'

'Sell by date excuse.'

'Well it would be rude not to then wouldn't it.'

'Absofuckinglutely.' Laughed Charlie ripping the croissant in half and passed it across to Alice who had already opened her laptop on the coffee table, a map showing on the screen and a frown on her forehead.

'Thanks love, do you mind if I have a play around for a bit? While it's all fresh in my mind?'

'Nah, go for it, I'll just finish this and go have a shower, shout if you want me.' Said Charlie heading off upstairs, tea in hand and half a croissant in her mouth.

Alice looked at her and smiled. *God she loved her.*

To be honest, finding the stone and the names on it the previous day had been firm in her mind, she just wanted to get the bare bones of the idea down on paper so they wouldn't be lost to the menopause mush. She'd already emailed the photos she'd taken to herself and had found the area on the old maps from 1851. The wrecked building was called Mill House and below it on the map there was another building roughly where the pile of stones were called Langdale Mill where she'd found the names. A quick google had brought up an old article written about the formation of the reservoir and that stones from the mill buildings had been reused as walling around it and as boundaries around the area.

Alice wondered, could the stone have come from the mill? Could the names be of girls who had worked there? She got shivers down her spine, the same feelings she had when she'd found the tin box under the floorboards the previous year. There was a mystery to be solved but she knew that she had to be patient for the archives to open in the New Year to properly get her teeth into it. She'd never get an appointment before Christmas closure.

Charlie came back into the living room, seeing Alice hunched over her laptop, her tongue sticking out the side of her mouth which she did when she was concentrating. She smiled.

'How ya getting on?'

'Not bad, just piecing things together on the map, I'm wondering if the names are of girls who worked there Charlie, you know, when it was a mill.'

'Wow how cool would that be! Quite the lucky find, what next?'

Alice frowned. 'Wait until everything opens up in the New Year I guess. I could have a look for the girls names and see what I can find. What time does Henry's 900th party of the month start?'

'We have to be at The Grand for 7, do you want me to drive in or get a taxi' replied Charlie, 'Jen and Holly are meeting us there.'

'We could always walk?' suggested Alice.

'We could, but.....it'll be cold.'

'Yes but won't a nice walk warm us up?'

'Think the dancing will take care of that. Will you be wearing heels? Might be icy?'

'What are you going to wear, thought I'd wear my big black number,' laughed Alice.

'Going full on posh, got my tux dry cleaned all ready.'

'With cufflinks?' asked Alice excitedly, she had a thing about cufflinks which made her knees go weak.

'Of course. You've never seen me in my tux have you?'

'No,' said Alice quietly. 'God am I going to be able to walk after I see you in it? We better get that taxi.'

Charlie laughed. 'Right, this isn't getting your work done and I'm distracting you. I'm going to make some soup for lunch to use up the veg, that ok? I feel so bloated and I bet the food tonight will be something else,' she said rubbing her slightly distended belly.

'Need a hand?' asked Alice half-heartedly, knowing damn well that Charlie was the better cook of the two of them.

'No, all's good, you crack on love,' she said giving her a kiss on the top of her head, Alice looked up and smiled at her. 'Have fun.'

So for the rest of the morning Alice buried herself in genealogy websites, making notes of potential people, her research made easier because of the girls unusual surnames. She found their births in Elvington near York, and then entry records for the workhouse too. From her previous research she'd read of workhouse children being removed to work in the mills in West Yorkshire and she wondered if she'd actually found two firm cases which was a researchers dream. She plotted the workhouse information onto Excel, she did love a spreadsheet.

Admission Book					
Names	Age	Last Address before admission	Condition	Calling	If able bodied
Dagnell Jane	31	Eastfield Cottages, Elvington	Widower	Char woman	Y
Dagnell Eliza	10	~ditto~	Scholar	~~~~~~~~	Y
Marr Ruth	29	~ditto~	Widower	Char Woman	Y
Marr Gertrude	10	~ditto~	Scholar	~~~~~~~~	Y

It was an added bonus to find the mothers names too so she jotted it all down for when she could get into the archives. She was so totally lost in her work that she didn't hear Charlie come back into the room.

'Two soups madam,' she joked, doing a comedy walk as she came in with the bowls.

Alice creased up laughing. 'Bloody hell, I nearly wet myself,' she said crossing her legs. 'I love that sketch.'

'Me too, grubs up,' she said putting the bowls on the coffee table.

'Mmmm smells gorgeous, god I feel I've ballooned 12 dress sizes. You may have to roll me out to the taxi. I have five parties with work in the next two weeks'

Charlie smiled, puffing out her cheeks. 'Definitely need to cut back, salads all round after Christmas' she said laughing.

'Good luck with that!'

They both sat on the sofa, sipping the soup slowly, but within minutes of finishing they were both yawning.

'Come on lass, get your coat on, let's go for a quick walk round by the river and wake ourselves up. We've got ages yet.' She pulled a reluctant Alice up. 'See it's your turn to resist exercise today.'

'True, do I get a bonus later then?' Alice smiled.

'Always,' said Charlie slapping Alice's bum as she walked past.

'Cheeky,' she laughed.

It was pleasantly mild and their swift walk was more of a shuffle, come amble but it felt good to be outdoors again. There weren't many people about other than the occasional runner. Lots of loud huffing and puffing announced their arrival. They nodded at each one passing then burst into laughter a few seconds later.

'If I'm ever seen running, you know I'm in danger so call the police,' Charlie joked.

'Ditto.' replied Alice, feeling much better for being outdoors for a while.

Returning to Alice's house, they decided on having a nap before getting ready for the party. This inevitably ended with an afternoon of glorious sex.

Sitting up in bed afterwards Alice looked at her phone to check the time.

'Shit, it's nearly half five, we better get up, what time's the taxi coming?'

'Booked for 6.45, come on gorgeous let's get this show on the road,' Charlie said patting Alice's bum.

'Yes boss,' said Alice swinging her legs out of bed. 'Do you want the bathroom first?'

'Nah, tux is at mine so gonna shower there, pick you up like old times at 6.40?' Charlie said taking a warm and snuggly Alice into her arms.

'That sounds perfect, can't wait to see you in your tux darling. See you soon,' Alice said giving her a quick peck on the cheek and scurried into the bathroom as Charlie headed next door.

After a short but lovely soak in the bath Alice blow dried her hair and readied herself, applying a small amount of makeup and put on a long black dress which had sparkles around the low-cut neckline. She had new black underwear underneath, that would be a nice surprise for Charlie later she thought. Putting on a pair of low-heeled shoes with a large silver buckle she looked at herself in the mirror hoping that she wouldn't let the side down.

Promptly at 6.40 Charlie rang the doorbell. She was suited and booted and her new silver knot cufflinks contrasted with her black tux. She was wearing the aftershave that Alice loved, that always made her go weak at the knees. As soon as she opened the door she saw in her eyes the desired effect, Alice looked stunning, and the thing was she didn't even know it. She had no idea how beautiful she was both inside and out.

'Wow, you look amazing, come here, let me smudge that perfect lipstick,' Charlie said taking Alice in her arms.

'Don't you dare, I don't want to turn up looking like Robert Smith, plus it's not your colour,' she replied cheekily, wriggling out of Charlie's arms. 'Let me grab Henry's card.'

Just then there was a beep from outside as the taxi arrived, so quickly putting on her long black coat from the peg in the hall they both got into the car and headed off to The Grand.

Arriving at the venue they were greeted by their friend Grace who was also sporting a tux, she looked so tired and Alice immediately knew that she was forcing the smile on her face. Jen and Holly were sat in chairs in the long corridor and seeing the threesome arrive they walked over.

'Where's the birthday boy?' asked Charlie.

'They've got a suite in the hotel so they'll be down soon I'd think,' said Grace. 'Everyone ready to party? I had a look in the room we're in and they've really thrown the chequebook at his birthday, it all looks incredible.'

Alice looked around the foyer, a large Christmas tree stood elegantly in the corner, beautifully adorned with delicate baubles and lights.

'I was feeling quite Bah Humbug about Christmas but this could definitely change my mind,' said Charlie. 'Shall we go through,' she said offering her arm to Alice.

'Well thank you kind woman, lead on,' giggled Alice as the five women headed into the ballroom where a waiter offered them a glass of champagne or orange juice as they entered.

Inside were many large round tables with the crispest white linen cloths and red and gold flowers in the centre of each. The tables framed a wooden dancefloor and a young female DJ stood before a very technical looking display. Another Christmas tree twinkled in the corner.

'Wow. It's so pretty,' said Holly. 'Do you think we'll have parties like this for our 60th's? It'll be upon us in no time at all.'

'Speak for yourself,' said Jen. 'I plan on working backwards now, soon be 21 again.'

Holly laughed. 'Would anyone really want to be 21 again? Remember how skint we were, the awful flats?'

'God yea, forgot about that,' said Jen.

Suddenly the room hushed and the DJ spoke.

'Put your hands together for the birthday boy Henry, congratulations on your big day.'

The room erupted with applause and Henry, accompanied by a beaming Lou came into the room who was wearing a floor length sparling black and silver dress. The DJ played Happy Birthday and the room sang to Henry. Quickly they looked at the seating plan and found their table, however after sitting there was a noticeable space next to Grace.

Grace broke the ice. 'Helen isn't coming. We broke up again last night. She didn't want to come tonight.'

'Because of what a cow she was the last time we were here?' asked Jen who voiced what everyone else was thinking.

'Kind of yes, she wanted Alice to apologise, she kept bringing it up. I don't know what to do. She buggers off then comes back again nice as pie. I can't think straight.'

'Fucking hell Grace,' said Jen. 'What a head fuck.'

Grace, her face pale with dark circles under her teary eyes took a tissue out of her pocket and dabbed her face dry.

'I know it's hard to stay away but do you know why you go back?' asked Holly.

'I don't know, she usually messages or emails with some crappy pretence about something at work, or tickets we have for something. I want her to stop. It's hurting so much,' replied Grace looking down at her hands which were clenched on the table.

'I don't know what to suggest, but it sounds so toxic,' said Holly. 'You deserve better.'

'I know. How do I stop this? How can I stop wanting to go back?'

Charlie who had sat patiently listening leant forward, placing her hands on Grace's. 'You've got to remember the bad things first, forget the good bits, the sex etc. Remember how shit she has made you feel. How many nights you've not slept. It'll hurt like a bastard but it'll stop. Have you blocked her?'

'I do, but then I weaken and unblock her, it's my own fault, I just hate this.'

'You need to block her for you own sake,' said Alice. We're all here to support you, if you feel tempted, pick up the phone and ring us, not her. You can do this.'

Grace put on a smile. 'I'll try. Sorry for being a fuckwit.'

'You're not, she's just a narcissist. She'll lose interest and move onto her next woman soon enough, women like her always do,' said Holly. 'In the meantime we're all here for you.'

'Thank you.'

Just then Lou walked over to their table.

'Isn't it just lovely, they've really surpassed themselves tonight. Do you think Henry's enjoying it?'

Henry, glass in hand, was entertaining a group of middle-aged men at the other side of the room, his face beaming as he told a story with interjections of laughter from the small crowd.

'Certainly seems it, the room looks so festive,' said Alice. 'Almost gives me the Christmas spirit.'

'We loved your afternoon tea here the other month so I knew it was the perfect place for his party.'

'True, I remember when you said you'd booked it.'

'How are you doing Lou?' asked Holly. 'Any update from the hospital?'

'I had the biopsy and the results were inconclusive so they operated and removed the mass, it isn't cancer....I only found out this afternoon.'

'Oh god Lou, what a relief, what was it?' began Alice.

'It's something called lobal carcinoma, but it isnt cancer. It just means I need more regular checks in case it turns to cancer,' Lou said calmly.

'Oh my god, what a relief,' said Alice getting up and hugging her friend, the others joined in too, gently.

'And treatments?' asked Holly, forever the GP.

'Just regular mammograms and I have to keep a closer eye than I normally would,' Lou said beaming, 'We're so relieved.'

'Totally, the best outcome. What a relief,' said Holly.

Henry came over and put his arm around her. 'Heard the best news ever I see.'

They all concurred nodding, 'Totally,' they agreed.

'Food will be served soon, hope you enjoy it Jen, made sure it's not tiny portions just for you, so you don't have to go to the chip shop on the way home,' smiled Henry.

Jen laughed. 'Cheers mate, eternally grateful.'

'Right my darling, let's go sit and then we can all eat, think the waiters are chomping at the bit.'

Lou and Henry went and joined the people at their table, and the serving staff swung into action bringing out the starters, others pouring wine like a well-oiled machine.

Lou had certainly surpassed herself in organising the party. The food was amazing, the menu contained all of Henry's favourites including beef wellington and Eton Mess, the wine changed and flowed depending on what course they were eating and the conversation on the tables were full of laughter.

After the tables were cleared the disco began with a mix of 80's classics and some 70's rock for Henry who strutted his stuff like Mick Jagger to the amusement of his very stiff looking friends from London. They all had a boogey except their sad friend as the sadness that emitted from Grace could be felt from two tables away.

'Do you want to go somewhere quiet and talk?' asked Alice seeing her friend wasn't participating at all and looked thoroughly miserable. She'd tried so hard to wear a smile on her face, but with the tiredness the mask had slipped and it was clear to see how unhappy she was.

'I'm not much company, I think I'll just go back home, mum and dad are going away just after Christmas so there's a bit to sort before they do.'

'I don't want you to be alone Grace, come back with us, stay the night,'

'Thanks but I just need to be at home. I'm fine honestly, it'll be fine. Say goodbye to Lou and Henry.'

'My phone's always on, just ring if you need me ok.'

Grace nodded and hugging Alice and waving goodbye left the party.

'I hate to see her so sad, what can we do?' asked Holly.

'I've not got a clue. I guess it just takes time to get over something like that. I don't know what to do.'

'We just have to be there when she's ready to talk, and let's just hope that Helen stays away from her, I somehow doubt it, narcissists need to feed off people and she's found a willing victim in Grace.'

'I'd like to have a word with her and it wouldn't be fucking polite,' said Jen.

'Ditto sis,' concurred Charlie.

'I'm going over to do Lou's horses in the morning so I will drop in to see Grace after,' said Alice. 'Wish I'd realised how bad she was.'

'You weren't to know, none of us were. She'll be ok, we'll all make sure of that, I just hadn't realised how bad it'd got,' said Holly.

They all nodded sadly.

'I don't know about you but I'm knackered, how about we finish off and get off home love, get up early and go have breakfast with Grace?' suggested Charlie.

'Good plan sis. Count us in, can we stay at yours tonight?' asked Jen.

'Sure, I'll get us a taxi,' said Charlie taking out her phone and heading into the lobby to make a call.

Alice found Lou who was sat flagging in a corner.

'We're going to head off home, we can't party like we used to.'

'I totally agree, don't know what's got into me, I'm bloody knackered too. Guess it's delayed shock from the results and all this planning. Henry's having a ball though isn't he,' she said looking over to where Henry was still dancing his heart out to Brown Sugar.

'He certainly is, it's been an amazing night, thanks so much for inviting us, enjoy the rest of your night. Say goodnight from us, I don't want to disturb his dancing.'

'I'm worried he'll wipe someone out with his arm flailing,' laughed Lou. 'Glad you could come, safe trip home sweetheart.

After hugging her friend goodbye they all made their way to the lobby where they retrieved their coats and with only a short wait went out to the taxi. Snuggling next to Charlie on the back seat Alice looked out of the window at York in all its glory at night, the Minster illuminated, the Christmas lights outside Bootham Bar, it looked magical.

'We'll make sure Grace is ok won't we,' said Alice. 'Maybe she'll feel better after a good night's sleep?'

'I hope so too,' said Charlie. 'I really do.'

Chapter Nineteen – To control and deceive

Despite their late night they were all up with the lark, the morning air was crisp and the pavements sparkling with frost as they set off to Lou's. Charlie diverted the Jeep to the local bakery and returned to the car with Jen with pastries and cups of steaming coffee which she distributed to everyone.

Once at the yard Alice busied herself making buckets of breakfast for the horses, then once eaten she put on their rugs and headcollars and took each horse out in turn to the field. They were all sleepy eyed and docile, their breath emitting plumes of steam from their nostrils as they headed over to a bale of haylage in the middle of the field.

Charlie, Jen and Holly had stayed warm and cosy in the Jeep, none of them were remotely horsey, and Alice knew that Charlie was terrified of them. Once finished she washed her hands in the tack room sink, and waving to the car's occupants, they all headed to the annexe up the lane where Grace lived. There were lights on in the kitchen and two cars parked outside.

Knocking at the kitchen door she saw Grace, wrapped in a dressing gown emerge from her bedroom and over to open the door.

Charlie, two brown bags in hand raised them as the door opened. 'Breakfast is served madam,' she said as Grace stepped back and they all entered the lovely spacious barn.

'What the?' Grace stood mouth agape.

'We've come with breakfast and listening ears. We wanted to make sure you were ok,' said Holly smiling at the friend she'd known since medical school.

'I'm ok …… I'm not alone….please don't make a scene.'

'Oh god sorry, we thought….' Started Alice.

Just then Helen emerged from the bedroom wearing a long t-shirt and short pyjama bottoms, displaying unmistakably bed hair.

'The gangs all here I see,' said Helen. 'I wasn't expecting a welcome party.'

'What the f…….' began Jen, Holly putting her hand on her arm to stop her.

'We brought you some breakfast, I was just sorting the horses for Lou.'

'That's kind of you, Helen was here when I got back, we've sorted things out.'

'Are you ok?' asked Holly.

'Fine, don't worry, you really didn't have to go to all this trouble.'

'Well we've brought pastries if YOU fancy something,' stressed Charlie putting the bags on the island.

'I'm sorry but Helen is taking me out for breakfast, sorry you've come all this way and ......'

'Waste not want not,' said Helen diving into the bags, taking out a pain au chocolate and taking a huge bite.

'Oi they're for......' started Jen, but Charlie interjected.

'What's going on Helen, I'm not sure what bullshit you've told Grace this time, what the fuck are you playing at?'

'Charlie, please don't.....' said Grace.

'Fuck you, it's nothing to do with any of you. We're good aren't we Grace,' said Helen putting her arm around her shoulders and pulling her in towards her in an awkward embrace.

'Yes, everything's fine, please leave it, all's good.'

'Told you. Now if you don't mind I'm getting in the shower, got to get my girl out for breakfast, we won't keep you, thanks for the treats.'

'Don't you fucking .....' said Jen moving towards Helen but was held back by both Holly and Charlie. 'Are you sure you want us to go Grace?'

'I think it's for the best, I'm fine, just go please.'

'Will you ring me later?' asked Alice.

'Of course, we just need some space to sort things out properly don't we Helen.'

'Whatever. Now if you don't mind we'd like space to get ready,' said Helen opening the back door.

'Are you sure,' Alice asked Grace again who nodded with the smallest of smiles, her eyes did not echo the sentiment.

The four of them filed out of the house stunned getting into the Jeep.

'What do we do now?' asked Charlie. 'God the arrogance of the woman.'

'I guess we just wait. Unless someone has any better ideas?' asked Holly.

'Should we just sit here and see what happens?' suggested Alice.

'It might cause more problems, she said she'd ring you and if anything happens I'm sure she will,' said Holly. 'Are you ok to drop us at home Charlie, I've got to get ready for work tomorrow and have some Christmas shopping to do.'

'Sure, the big day approaches eh. What are you guys doing?' asked Charlie.

'Not sure, Madeline has been asking the same question. Do you both want to come to us? I'm sure she'd love both her daughters there and we came to yours last year, asked Holly.

'I was going to suggest the same. What do you think love?' asked Charlie. 'Sounds a nice plan, shall we ask Grace too?'

'Of course, although she'll probably be with her parents I think.'

'Well whatever happens let's try and have a good one eh,' said Charlie unconvincingly.'

As they left Askham Bryan Charlie took the long route back to the outer ring road, driving slowly past Ashfield Farm due to a tractor and trailer pulling out. The for-sale board was still outside. She still hadn't talked to Alice about her plan, there had been so much going on. She glanced sideways at Alice who was looking down the lane too.

'That's where my grandad used to work after he left Middleham when he couldn't be a jockey, it was part of the big Askham Richard estate, I didn't know it was for sale.'

'I didn't know that love, I know that you said that he worked in Askham Richard at one time. Did he live here too as well as work?' asked Charlie smiling inside.

'Yeah he told me that the grooms slept in the attic at first but when he became top groom he got his own bedroom,' she said laughing. 'He always said it was the first bed he'd had to himself. There were 17 of them in a 2-bed terrace house growing up, lots of bed sharing.'

'Wow, that's serious overcrowding, we don't know we're born do we,' said Holly.

'No we don't.'

Charlie carried on driving deep in thought. Ideas sparking in her head driving to Jen and Holly's house.

'Will you let me know if Grace rings?' asked Holly.

'Sure, I somehow doubt she will.'

'Have to say I agree with you,' said Jen. 'See you soon sis.'

Jen and Holly let themselves into their house and Charlie and Alice drove back home, both deep in thought for different reason.

Chapter Twenty – The Thrills but no Spills

The lead up to Christmas was manic, finishing off work, buying presents and works parties every long weekend. By the time the big day arrived both Charlie and Alice were frazzled. The relief of going to their friends for Christmas took the pressure off cooking and organising the meal, but there had been a sleepless night or two over what to buy Charlie's mum. They had only been in touch a year and although Jen gave some suggestions, their strained relationship had also led her into unknown territory too. Eventually they decided on taking her away on a family holiday to the coast at Easter and bought her a spa day at The Grand along with a Christmas stocking with toiletries and chocolates.

There had been no news from Grace at all, she hadn't replied to messages either. Lou said she'd seen her and Helen around a fair bit so they concluded that they'd sorted themselves out, and as they were all going to Lou and Henry's for Boxing Day they decided to see where the land lay then.

The big day passed with much laughter and fun. Presents were gratefully received and Jen had cooked up a storm in the kitchen. Madeline had enjoyed her presents too so waking on Boxing Day morning they all wore big smiles.

Madeline was already fully dressed and up sipping tea when they all came downstairs in their PJ's and slippers.

'You're an earlier bird than us mum,' said Jen. 'Everything ok?'

Putting down her cup onto the delicate porcelain saucer that Holly had bought her she poured herself another cup from the matching teapot.

'I'm volunteering with a York homeless charity today; my friend Hugo sent me a text to say they'd got a space if I'd like to help. Do you mind? Do you think Lou and Henry will be cross?' she said with a little hint of French accent.

'Of course not mum, that's very kind of you,' said Charlie. 'Do you want a lift there?'

'No I think I need a walk to be truthful, all this rich food, I'm very full still.'

'I've told Jen that next year we're going to a health spa, cabbage soup and fresh juice,' laughed Holly.

Madeline laughed.

'Absolutely, not sure why it feels worse this year?' said Charlie. 'I'm so bloated, think I have been for weeks.'

'I've had so many works do's I don't think I've stopped eating all December,' groaned Alice.

'Me too,' replied Holly readjusting her trousers. 'Nothing fits right anymore.'

Jen smiled at her patting her stomach. 'I'm good, I practice this all-year round.'

The five of them laughed.

'Do you think Henry will just have salads for us?'

'We can but hope,' said Charlie.

It was as they all feared when they got to Lou and Henry's later that day. They were greeted with canapes and glasses of champagne or fruit punch and the Aga was overflowing with pans as Henry cooked up another of his masterpieces. Lou was in good spirits quite literally; she was already tipsy when she let them in.

Charlie went to help Henry who was looking a tad stressed.

'Bloody hell what you cooking up today? Enough for the whole of York never mind the village,' she laughed.

'I got carried away with the peeling, didn't want anything to go to waste, Grace is coming over with her parents and Harriet and Clive are coming too.'

'Mmmm well you might need to spread that out a bit more Henry or we'll all be bursting.'

Alice smiled over at Charlie. God she loved her, that was a given, but sometimes she would look at her when she was distracted or working and feel such a rush of love and affection for her it was overwhelming. Charlie smiled back, then taking a tea towel she set about draining vegetables in the colander and putting them into the tureens on the island.

Just then there was a knock at the back door and a sheepish looking Grace and her parents arrived followed by Harriet and Clive.

'Come in, come in, get yourselves a drink,' said Henry whisking the gravy vigorously.

Jen handed them all a glass of champagne and took the canapes to them but they declined. Jen popped another into her mouth.

After making introductions and greetings, and with Henry suitably praised for his culinary skills they all mingled around the island.

'How was everyone's Christmas?' asked Grace.

'Knackering,' replied Jen. 'How can doing nothing but eat leave you absolutely fucked.'

Grace's parents visibly winced.

'You ok?' mouthed Alice to Grace who nodded and looked away.

'God knows, I feel ready to go back to work to get away from it all,' said Holly giving Jen a please mind your language cock of the head.

'Congratulations on your book Alice, I got a copy online, it was a great read, brilliant story,' said Harriet.

'Thanks that's really appreciated. I feel so blessed you've all supported me.'

'What have you got planned next? Are you working on anything at the minute.'

Just as Alice was about to answer Lou cleared her throat.

'Let's leave the chefs to it,' said Lou. 'Let's go through to the sitting room.'

'I'll be through in a minute,' said Holly. 'Just need to use the loo.'

They all went through to the sitting room leaving the two chefs to finish up dinner. Alice told them about her and Charlie's woodland adventure, well the PG version and the story of her two new case studies Eliza and Gertrude, the mill they worked at and the lives they might have lived there.

Harriet was super excited at the news, explaining that her family were from West Yorkshire originally and her great grandparents had all worked in the mills along with their children.

'Wow, that's amazing. What a spectacular find,' said Lou. 'What's next?'

'Into the archives and see what I can find out, it could turn into another academic paper or write another book maybe, I need to try and get some funding for field work, see where that goes. Next year looks exciting.'

'It does,' said Harriet. 'I've exciting news too. We've found a house, well a business really.'

'Brilliant,' said Lou. 'You kept that quiet! Where is it?'

'Just down the road from here in Askham Richard, it hasn't even gone live on the market, we were so lucky.'

'Who's lucky?' Asked Charlie entering the sitting room along with Holly.

'Harriet's found a house with business space near here,' said Alice smiling at her, she could visibly see her face fall.

'Er tell me more,' she said sitting on the chair arm next to Alice visibly stunned.

Harriet went into her bag and brought out the property details and handed them to Charlie who read them out. A smile spread across her face in relief.

'Stunning farmhouse in rural village, 5 beds, 4 bathrooms fully modernised with established business attached,' she flicked over the page eagerly. 'Outbuildings containing entertaining space, fully fitted industrial kitchen and accommodation. Currently run as 5* outside catering establishment. Two further Dutch barns with planning permission ripe for conversion to further business space. Stands in 25 acres with stable block and paddocks and floodlit arena. Looks bloody lovely Harriet, what are you going to do with it?'

'The plan is to obviously have the horses at home, sorry Lou,' she said smiling across at her friend. 'But then I'm not sure what else, which is what I'd like to talk through with you if that's ok Charlie?'

'Great, let's do that. Shit I was meant to tell you dinners ready but got distracted, but yes let's talk.' A large smile spread across her face.

Alice stood up to go through to the kitchen but quickly whispered in Charlie's ear 'God you're hot when you talk about stuff.'

Charlie smiled and taking her by the hand they went through for yet another dinner.

At the table Alice sat next to Grace on one side of her and Charlie on the other. Grace's parents, who to Alice seemed very refined and elegant were sat with Holly and Jen at the other end of the table. They looked concerned, finding a great deal of interest in their napkins and cutlery. Charlie was deep in conversation with Harriet, they both had their phones out, typing things into notes. Alice smiled turning to Grace, however her smile quickly turned to a frown.

'Are you ok?' she asked quietly, they'd not spoken since the day they'd all been round and Helen saw them out.

'Look, I'm really sorry about the other day and not messaging. Could we have a chat during the week? Don't want to bring the party down.'

'You could never do that but we can maybe ride out tomorrow if you wanted? I'm sure Lou wouldn't mind me borrowing Harvey.'

'How about a walk instead, I've lost my nerve a bit.'

'Ok we can do that no problem, when is good for you?'

'Do you want to come for 10, meet me at home?'

'Thanks, that'd be great. I'm off for a few days,' she said looking down at her uneaten food on her plate.

'You can tell me all about it tomorrow, but ring me tonight if you wanted?'

'Thanks, will see how late it is before we get finished here, I'm so very tired.'

'You look exhausted Grace, is it work?'

'No, work's ok, it's the rest of the shit show. I don't know what's wrong with me.'

'Look, shall we go outside now?'

'No I don't want my parents to worry, looks like they are having a bit of a culture shock at their end of the table,' she said smiling, looking at her mum fidgeting with her pearls, her dad looking like he wished he could hide amongst the melon balls in the dish in front of him.

'As long as you're sure, I'm here if you need me, we are all here for you.'

Grace smiled her thanks. Then looking at her bowl again she sighed heavily as she forced herself to eat something so as not to be rude.

'I'm so tired of food.'

'God me too, roll on New Years Day, my resolution is to go on a health kick and no more overindulging.'

'Mine is to sort my life out,' said Grace.

Alice frowned. 'We really need to talk don't we.'

Grace nodded.

'Of course, no problem,' said Alice making a note on her phone. On her other side Charlie was in and out of the kitchen carrying tureens and dishes of food and spreading them out onto the table with Lou and Henry.

God she really is hot thought Alice just as Charlie looked across at her, a wide grin across her face. Damn it she knew exactly what she was thinking. Charlie sat down and everyone tucked into yet another Christmas dinner. They all pulled crackers, toasts were made and there was a lot of laughter from all except Grace who it was clear to see was wearing a hard smile. Her eyes were down, not making much eye contact at all.

Further up the table laughter broke out, Grace was relieved of the distraction and turning to look she saw her mum pulling a cracker with Jen, wearing a paper hat awkwardly crooked, her dad looking on with a stunned look on his face as Jen was in hysterics.

'Pull it woman, use ya muscles' bellowed Jen.

Grace's mum used both hands to pull the cracker, falling hard onto the back of her chair as she won the duff end. Jen elated at winning unpacked the cracker retrieving a hat of her own and a tape measure.

'Ready for the joke,' she said pulling out a slip of paper. 'Who hides in a bakery at Christmas?'

Grace's mum shook her head, 'No idea who hides in a bakery at Christmas?'

'A mince spy,' said Jen bursting into laughter again.

There were giggles from around the table, and Grace's parents let out a nervous laugh.

'Rubbish aren't they, maybe I should write my own,' laughed Jen.

'Good plan Jen, they couldn't be worse than these,' agreed Henry who started to clear the table, Charlie stood up and helped as did Lou. There was a lot of food left. 'Think there will be Tupperware presents for all of you if you wanted to make some bubble and squeak tomorrow?'

There were audible groans around the table.

'Maybe just freeze it Henry, think everyone is fooded out.' Said Lou.

There were many nods from their guests.

After the plates were cleared and only Jen helped herself to a Tupperware box and a big piece of Christmas cake, they played a quick game of charades and decided to call it a night. The mood could be summed up as jaded.

'Next year it's salads all round,' said Henry.

'Next year let's all go to a health spa,' suggested Lou. 'I feel decidedly sick.'

'Bless you, the spa sounds like a good plan, it will be here in the blink of an eye, does anyone else feel the years are just speeding up?' said Grace.

'Totally, when we were teenagers a month seemed to go on for years didn't they Lou?' replied Alice.

'They did, we didn't have many cares in the world did we,' said Lou, then realising what she had said she stroked Alice's arm. 'Sorry, I wasn't thinking, your mum made things so hard for you, sorry I forgot for a minute.'

'It's ok, it past and gone, it's the present and future that matters now,' she said looking adoringly at Charlie across the room who was helping Henry load the dishwasher. *God she loved her, how could you love someone so much that you felt your heart would burst? She thought.*

'So true, come on Charlie let me do that, you get yourselves home, it's been so lovely to see you all,' said Lou all teary eyed.

Alice gave her a big hug and Grace came forward and hugged her too. 'See you tomorrow,' she said quietly.

Everyone got into their cars and Charlie took the wheel to drive them home.

'Tell me more about the girls at the mill you found, I caught snippets of it when I came back from the loo,' asked Holly from the back seat.

'I only know a little so far, I need to get into the archives and to look into their family's details and to find out more about the mill. Those poor kids had a very hard life. Doesn't it make you feel so grateful for what we have now.'

'It really does, but if anyone can bring their stories to life again it's you Alice,' said Holly. 'I absolutely know it will be you.'

Chapter Twenty-One – Waiting for the axe to fall

The following morning Alice kissed Charlie goodbye and headed back to Askham Bryan and Grace's house. Being after Christmas the tourist levels had dropped and the sales hadn't properly started so her journey was quick and painless. Since being with Charlie her anxiety had pretty much disappeared, the safety and security she felt had calmed her so much. She felt so blessed.

Thoughts of Grace brought her back from her little fantasy world she was building in her head as she drove. She had seemed so happy in summer after meeting Helen, however the weirdness on the book signing day had been very odd and out of the blue and then the other week when they were escorted out of the house. Maybe Helen was just insecure and it came out sideways into blaming her of cheating, although the way Grace had been so unhappy of late she worried that it had all gone too far. It was all very difficult.

Alice parked behind the annexe and knocked on the door. A very weary Grace answered the door, large dark circles very apparent under her eyes.

Entering the annexe, which was normally so neat and tidy in a minimalist style, was today cluttered, opened and unopened mail on each surface, Christmas wrapping paper rolls and Sellotape on the floor, scissors and ribbons, and a pile of presents unopened lay on the kitchen table.

'Tea?' asked Grace.

'Please,' replied Alice looking for a place to sit. Newspapers were strewn across the sofa and washing piled on the chairs. So gingerly picking her way across the floor she folded the papers and set them on the coffee table.

Grace, coming over with two mugs set them down on top of the newspapers.

'Sorry for the mess, I've not been myself. Just can't seem to motivate myself lately. Would you like a biscuit?' she asked about to stand up again,

'No, I couldn't eat another thing, I'm still stuffed from last night.'

'Henry brought 2 lots of Tupperware over this morning that were left over from last night as he couldn't get them in the freezer. It's very kind but don't think I can eat it either.'

'Bless you, we're the same, it's all been a bit much hasn't it, there seem to have been a million events this year. Have you had loads too?'

'There have been yes, but I didn't go to any this year.'

'Why's that?'

'Helen would have been at most of them, and the others she might have been. We broke up again.'

'When did that happen?'

'A couple of days ago, I just felt so embarrassed, it's been hell to be honest. Constantly fighting and just awful.'

'Fighting about what? I am sorry to hear that.'

'Same old, same old. Thinking that you and I were having an affair, that I was cheating on her with a colleague at work, you name it, I had no peace, I'm just so tired.'

'That is totally ridiculous. There's never been anything between us, she knows I'm with Charlie. I don't understand.'

'Me neither, she just doesn't believe whatever I say, it's really getting me down.'

'You said you've had time off work?'

'I called in sick, I had to, I couldn't think straight, I was up and down all the time and I have to focus so hard in my job, it was safer to be off sick than make mistakes.'

'I understand. How long are you off for?'

'Another few weeks. I don't know if I can face it. I have loved my job for so long, but now, I just can't wait to finish, to get home, I don't care anymore. Maybe it's time to call it a day.'

'Don't do anything hasty Grace. Have you talked to your mum and dad about it?'

'No, they've gone on their winter holiday early this morning, they are going down the Nile but first on the Orient Express, the full Agatha Christie experience.'

'Wow, sounds amazing, do you want to come and stay with us for a while? You'd be very welcome.'

'I just want to be on my own, I'm awful company, I can't stop crying, pathetic eh. Plus I have to be here for my parents dog, mums best friend is collecting her in the morning.'

' Ah I see ok. You're not pathetic at all. Remember how I was when I broke up with Charlie, we hadn't been together as long as you two, you have to give yourself time to grieve.'

'She's coming here later to pick up her stuff, I offered to drop it off at her house but she said she'd come here. I'm dreading it but I so want to see her too.'

'What time is she coming? Do you want me to stay whilst she comes?'

'She's coming at 6, but it's ok, I just want to be on my own, I have to clean up and decide if I'm giving her the presents I bought her,' said Grace pointing to the pile of unopened presents.

'It would be very generous to give her them, but if she's been treating you so badly is it right to do that?'

'I don't honestly know; it's all been so confusing. Maybe I am too fucked up like she said.'

'What do you mean?'

'She says I am always triggered, that I'm a mess. That I make up arguments. I don't know if I'm on my head or my heels.'

'Sounds really awful, I think when we get to our 50's we all have triggers, we've all been through so much crap we're bound to. It's what we do with that.'

'Thing is I don't think I have, after we fight I don't know where I am, my head is spinning and I just want to run away. She hangs up on me and won't talk to me for days, I try ending it and walking away but she drags me back in again. I just can't cope. I feel like a bad person all the time,' Grace said, her eyes full of tears, staring at the opposite wall.

'No one should make you feel like that, it's not on. If it's not working then have a grown-up conversation and move on. Don't torture the person you're supposed to care about.'

'That's just what it feels like, torture. Maybe she is right, I shouldn't have started this.'

'But you didn't start 'this,' said Alice feeling agitated. 'She asked you out at the Tod disco, not the other way around. She pursued you that night and bombarded you with texts, it was so like love bombing.'

Grace frowned. 'Love bombing? Do you think so?'

Alice paused, not knowing what to say, should she say that Charlie had thought so too.

'Ok, please don't get mad, but Charlie said something right at the beginning that she thought it was a bit much. Full on. But you seemed so happy and didn't seem to mind the number of times she was messaging. We don't feel we know her though; she's put a distance between us all because of saying she thinks we are having a fling. That isn't right Grace.'

'I hadn't thought of that, she's said she doesn't like anyone of the group, but I thought that was just her personality, might be too shy to try and integrate with us all being close friends. I thought she'd come round and want to try knowing how important you all are to me.'

'But instead she's made things even more awkward by accusing you, and then you won't bring her to things because of that. She's got you over a barrel. Do you want to start things with her again? Is that what you're going to say to her today?'

'I truly don't know. I just want peace. I feel so confused. I've never had depression, I've been so lucky not to have had anxiety, I've always been confident in my work. But lately I don't know up from down. I wake up so often in the night there isn't much point going to bed, it's why I took time off. I just feel so bad. Maybe it's just hormonal, maybe Helen is right, I'm not right in the head.'

'Hey, I won't hear a word of that Grace. There's nothing wrong with you. She's playing with your head. She seems to be taking pleasure in it too. Please let me stay whilst she's here, I can go and come back later, or I can stay and we can go out for a walk?'

'Let's go out for a walk, it might help to clear my head a bit maybe. Let me get my shoes on,' she said getting up and went into her bedroom.

Alice could see that the bed was unmade and there were clothes on the floor in piles. Getting her phone out she texted Charlie to let her know she would be longer than she'd said at which point Grace appeared and they headed out into the chilly winter air.

The paths were still a little icy and there was frost on the grass verges as they walked up the village and onto a bridleway which took them both across open fields, over hedges with stiles and around the edge of Askham Richard. They lost their way for a little while but found the track again which looped round and back to the annexe. Grace was silent for most of the walk, occasionally stopping to look at the view or to point something out, but the most part of it she was quiet and deep in thought. Alice, walking as fast as she could was struggling and was grateful that Grace stopped to look at things or to make a brief conversation which masked how out of breath she was, thankfully she was too distracted to notice too much.

'You ok?' she asked as they neared the annexe.

'Don't worry about me, I'm good. Did the walk help?'

'It did a bit yes. Now I don't want to be rude but I'm going to crack on with my housework, I've got a bit behind, I don't want Helen to see how I am really.'

'I can stay and ....'

'No it's ok. I can manage. I made the mess I need to clear it up. Anyway it'll fill in the time won't it.'

'Ok, as long as you're sure. I'll call you later if that' ok?'

'You don't need to. I'm ok.'

Giving Grace a hug Alice got back into her car and headed back home. She was worried about her but knew she couldn't have insisted on staying. Or could she.

Arriving home she found Charlie in her office, one screen showing a wedding site and the other screen with a spreadsheet.

'How was Grace? Didn't she want to come back with you?'

'No she wouldn't, she's got Helen coming round later to collect her things. She's in a bad way Charlie. Not herself at all. Helen sounds a proper bitch, even more than we have witnessed so far.'

Charlie looked taken aback.

'Wow, I've never heard you say that about anyone! What has she done?'

Alice gave Charlie a brief idea of what had gone on. She was visibly shocked.

'I think we should go over there and have a word with Helen. That really isn't on. You don't treat someone like that, and I know that sounds shite coming from me.'

'It was different though with you wasn't it, you didn't play games, you were up front. Women catch feelings, it's what we do. That wasn't your fault, you didn't keep them hanging on and saying cruel things to them did you?'

'No, but you know I still feel awful about it all. Anyway what are we going to do about Grace?'

'I don't know, she wanted to deal with it herself, I said I'd ring her later to make sure all was ok. I hope she doesn't take her back; you don't think she will do you?'

'She might, she's a grown woman and knows her own mind, we can see what's happening but sometimes you have to hit rock bottom to understand what is right under your nose. It's really tough I know, let's see how she gets on love, try not to worry.'

Alice headed back downstairs, her head addled, she couldn't focus on anything but what was going on with Grace. She hoped for the best but she had a bad feeling in her gut.

Chapter Twenty-Two – A race against time

That evening, sitting quietly and comfortably on the sofa in Alice's living room, the log burner kicking out some romantic flames as Charlie ran her fingers through Alice's long hair, untangling it gently as she rested her head on her lap.

'Penny for your thoughts,' said Charlie looking down at Alice's eyes with the reflection of the fire dancing in them.

'Sorry love, I was just thinking about Grace. I'm really worried about her. I invited her to come and stay with us but she said no, but I think I should invite her again, what do you think? Would you mind if we invited her to stay for a couple of days? She said she's off sick, she never goes sick Charlie. Something isn't right,' said Alice rambling, her words jumbled.

'Calm down sweetheart,' said Charlie. 'Yeah she's a workaholic like we are. Give her a ring, I've nowt on if you have to work I can hang out with her.'

'Thanks love,' said Alice getting her phone and ringing her number. Getting no reply Alice typed out a message. 'I've got a bad feeling Charlie; I think I'm going to drive over.'

'We'll both go, don't worry I'm sure she's fine. Ring Lou, see if her car is there, she should be able to see from her house?'

Alice dialled Lou.

'No reply, let's just go and see,' said Alice putting on her boots and grabbing her coat from the hall.

Charlie got ready and they headed out the door. It was a cold night; the Jeep windscreen was a little frosted but cleared quickly. The roads to Askham Bryan were free of traffic but when they pulled into the lane Grace's car was nowhere to be seen. There was a light on at Lou's so they parked next to Henry's sports car and knocked on the back door.

The door was opened by Lou.

'Hi, what a lovely surprise, we didn't have plans did we?'

'No don't worry. Have you seen Grace this evening? I'm worried about her; she was really upset when we went for a walk this morning. Has she said anything to you?'

'About Helen? Yes briefly, she came over an hour ago and gave us the keys for her parents' house to let Maisie out and so that their friends can collect her in the morning. Henry told her to call it a day with Helen but I don't know if she has, she just said she was going away for the night.'

'Did you know that she's gone off sick, it's just not like her. I just got a feeling from her that something's really wrong but she wouldn't tell me everything.'

'Er..... let me have a look on my phone, we have this app for when we go out riding on our own so we always know where we are in case of an accident.' Lou got out her phone and found the app. 'Ok she's driving, she's on the A64 near Malton, she's going really fast,' she said showing the phone to Charlie which showed Grace going over 70 mph.

'Can you add us to the app? I think we need to follow her,' said Alice anxiously. 'I've got a really bad feeling.'

'Charlie can you see if you can do that, Henry set it up for me and he's at a meeting in York.'

Taking the phone Charlie added herself to the app which then showed where they all were, including a speeding Grace.

'Ok we'd better go; we'll ring when we know more,' said Alice as they both headed back to the Jeep.

'She's about 20 mins ahead of us,' said Alice, putting the phone on charge. 'She's still on the A64.'

'Does she know anyone out that way?'

'I don't think so, as far as I know her parents are her only family. Helen lives near Selby somewhere.'

They drove at speed, the traffic non-existent, sensible people staying at home. Alice kept an eye on the phone app, Grace still moving fast.

'She's just turned off towards Filey, I think I know where she's heading. She told me the other week that she and Helen went to Flamborough the other month and she'd never felt so happy sat with her there. Think we should ring the police or someone?'

'Definitely, I'll put my foot down,'

Alice rang 999 and after a few rings it was answered. She went through what had happened, how worried she was and gave directions of where they were heading, assuring them she was the passenger not the driver. She answered questions about what her car was like, what Grace looked like as they sped through the night.

'She's pulled into the clifftop car park I can see she's stopped. We're about 20 mins behind her roughly, can you send someone, please,' begged Alice and was assured that they were sending someone and contacting the coastguard. They stayed on the line whilst Charlie drove like the wind along main roads then off onto the country road, Alice directing her until driving down the long Marine Drive they saw Grace's car parked ahead, the place in darkness, her car highlighted by the full moon above with no sign of life.

Chapter Twenty-Three – At Last There's Peace

It had been a hard day since Alice had left. Grace had tidied and cleaned and decided to give the presents to Helen. She'd put a lot of thought into them, the first edition of her favourite book, chocolates and tickets to see a band that she'd always wanted to see including a hotel stay to go with it with a spa. She knew she'd love it. But why didn't Helen love her? Was she really that unlovable? Her overthinking brain wrapping itself in knots as the day ticked on. As the time of Helen's arrival approached her nerves were at the highest they had ever been and she had thrown up a couple of times. She'd cried a lot and really hoped that she was all cried out and would be strong when she saw her again.

She'd collected together all the bits and pieces that Helen had left at hers, the toiletries, the t-shirt she'd left there for her with her scent on it that she had cuddled in the dark hours. She could smell it so strongly as she had packed them into a box. The PJ's with the Christmas design that they had said they would wear as a matching set on the big day. That had never happened. So much had never happened from promises Helen had made. Grace felt physically and mentally drained and wobbly, she hadn't eaten all day, in fact the only decent meal she had had in a while had been at the meal she had picked at the day before.

Just as she was lost in thought there was a knock at the door. Thinking it was too early and that Lou must want something she answered it, however there stood Helen, dressed in her going out to impress suit. The collar turned up, her short hair had been recently cut and she looked as gorgeous as the first time she had really got to know her at the Tod disco.

'Helen? Er come in, you're early.'

'Wanted to get it out of the way, I'm out tonight.'

'Oh ok, do you want a cup of tea? Coffee?'

'No I can't stop; I've got a date.'

'A date? We literally broke up a few days ago!'

'Yeah but like I kept telling you, we weren't a **thing**,' Helen said using her fingers on both hands to exaggerate the last word. 'Don't look at me like that. I told you so many times, you just didn't listen. Anyway I got sick of you cheating, or if you aren't now you certainly will be soon. I know you Grace, you're a piece of work. You pretend to be all sweet and kind and all things to all women, but really you're just a sly bitch. I hope Charlie is keeping a close eye on you.'

'I'm not……I'm not like that. I never could cheat on anyone. I only ever wanted to be with you.'

'Bullshit. I know what Charlie's reputation is, maybe they are just very alike her and Alice, is it an open relationship or have they got a poly thing going on?'

'Please stop, you've got it so wrong, Helen please. It's not like that, it never ever was I promise you.'

'I'm not blind, your denial is just crap. I don't think you know what the truth is anymore. You clung so tight to me I thought I would suffocate, you need to get a grip, you're a grown woman, no one wants to be with someone like that. Not sure why I asked you out in the first place.'

'That's cruel Helen, please stop. Look here's your things, and the presents I got you for Christmas. I want you to have them to enjoy. But please stop. We have to work together; we can't have this atmosphere when we see each other.'

'I'm going to make sure we never ever work together again. I'll tell them how possessive you've been and your behaviour, I'll make sure that we never see each other.'

'You'll ruin me, you can't do that to me, all I ever did was love you. I don't deserve this. You know I never did any of those things. Please Helen. Let's just part as friends, there's no need to go down this path. Let's just take a break.'

'You're delusional. I don't want to be your friend. Why the fuck would I want that? You mean nothing to me, you never did. Now the lass I'm taking out tonight, well she's a keeper, she doesn't have hang ups, she's not frigid. She's not an embarrassment like you, god I don't know what I was thinking. You can keep your shitty presents, and the rest of my stuff just chuck it, I don't want it back.'

'Then why come today? What was the point?'

'Dunno, just wanted to tell you in person what I think of you, might be worth you looking for another job, I'm going to finish you, no one makes a fool out of me,' said Helen her eyes flashing dangerously.

'I've........'

'Oh shut up. I've nothing else to say to you. Just never contact me again.'

Helen turned and walked out leaving the door wide open. Grace stood completely stunned in the kitchen, a mug still in her hand from when Helen had arrived. She shook from head to toe. Her fingers let go of the mug which smashed to the ground.

The dark cloud which had been following her around for months descended around her. She felt a heavy thud of grief in the pit of her stomach, all she could hear was her brain telling her to get out of there, to drive, to get as far away as possible. The desire for peace, for quiet, to escape from the voice in her head that told her enough was enough. That the time had come, what was the point in carrying on anymore. Why stay where she wasn't wanted, where her life was ruined, both her personal life and her job, the place she loved. The people she loved but would soon tire of her.

So locking up she told her friend and neighbour Lou that she was going away urgently and to look after Maisie. Then getting into her car she headed to the coastline where she felt most alive. Where she knew she had to go. To finish it all.

She'd cried the whole hours' drive, with no cars on the road she'd put her foot down and broken many speed restrictions, but at this point she really didn't care. Music blaring all the way she knew what her objective was which gave her a sense of calm. It would all soon be over, she would no longer be in pain, no longer a disappointment, no longer unloved.

Grace pulled into the car park, it was dark and the local pub was closed, the cliffs were illuminated by the full moon on the wintry night. Parking her old MG nearest the cliff she sat staring at the sea for a little while, admiring its beauty, knowing this was the last thing that she would ever see.

She got out of the car, automatically putting the key into her pocket she took off her jacket and lay it on the driver's seat, she'd always liked the coat and hoped that someone would get the benefit of it when she was gone. She did the same with her jumper and scarf, removing her shoes and placed them on top. She closed the door for the final time, she loved that car so much but none of it mattered anymore. She didn't want anything. Her heart was broken, she felt as though her whole world had caved in and dark shadows followed her around that completely enveloped her. She no longer saw the brightness in anything, she just wanted it all gone.

Memories of Helen flooded her mind, how she'd allowed someone into her life, into her heart and she'd used everything she'd ever told her against her. All of her fears, her hopes, she'd dangled under her nose, pulling it away as it got close. Promises of a future together, dreams of what could have been. She'd mourned her, she'd cried over her but the pain never eased, the blackness was so deeply etched into her soul there was no coming back from it.

So wearing just her shorts and T-shirt she walked to the benches along the cliff top. She sat down on the one furthest from the car park, away from potentially being seen. The frost on the wood soaked the fabric on her legs which were already turning red from the extreme cold.

Grace had planned this for a while, she'd thought of what way out she could take. Being a doctor she had access to everything, but she didn't want to cause problems for the hospital nor the pharmacy and she knew she wanted a nonviolent end. Knowing how fast hypothermia took hold, especially in the icy sea air it wouldn't take long for her body to shut down. Laying on the bench, curling her legs up she looked out over the bay, hearing the sea crashing against the shore and rocks, it was so peaceful. At first it was painful, the cold biting deep into her flesh and bones, shivering and her breathing initially fast was slowing down as she knew it would as everything within her shut down.

She thought about Helen, why had she treated her so badly, was she a bad person, had she taken pleasure in watching her suffer? Had she taken delight at how open she was to everything that she'd wanted but shut Grace down when she made a suggestion and was made to feel as though she was a failure, not good enough and someone she could use. And use her she had. She'd pushed her through every emotion, every kindness within her she felt was unreal, that she was the worst woman ever to walk the planet. She'd never known how Helen felt, she'd never said. Grace had just persevered hoping that she would hear I love you repeated back to her. She knew now that it never would. That she would never hear those words again from anyone.

The shivering had stopped, her breathing had slowed, the clouds above covered the moon, everything getting darker, she closed her eyes for the final time, allowing the feeling of sleep to overtake her. Her final thoughts of how peaceful she felt that it was all over now, she could just sleep listening to the waves and the wind that swirled around her. Peace approached at last.

Chapter Twenty-Four – It ain't over til it's over

Everything was a blur. Alice remembered Charlie turning fast into the carpark. Braking heavily and jumping out to look inside Grace's car, there was no sign of her in there, her coat and clothes piled on the seat inside. Then going into the boot of the Jeep she got out a big torch and they both headed out towards the clifftop.

It was Charlie who spotted Grace first, laid on the bench on top of the cliff.

Shouting at Alice, her voice just about audible above the crashing waves below and the wind howling around the cliff. All the while on the phone to the emergency services who assured her that help was nearly there, as she relayed to them where Grace was.

'Get the car nearer,' she said passing her car keys to Alice. 'Bring the blankets and keep the heater on.'

Alice drove the Jeep as close as she could to the bench, jumping out and getting the blankets from the boot she opened the passenger door as Charlie approached carrying Grace. Putting an unconscious Grace in the passenger seat they wrapped her in blankets and the heat was on full.

They both jumped into the car and closed the doors to keep the heat in, Charlie in the front and Alice in the back.

'Oh god Grace, what have you done,' said Charlie stroking her hair. She didn't make a sound; they couldn't hear her breathing and nor could they feel a pulse.

Just then blue flashing lights could be seen in the distance bouncing off the clouds above.

'Help is here Grace, hang on please,' pleaded Alice.

Charlie got out and ran to the road to wave the ambulance into the car park. Pulling up beside the Jeep they took over, asking for her name, age and address whilst moving Grace to the ambulance, where they wrapped her in heated blankets, and placed packs under her arms and between her legs. They listened for a heartbeat, which they announced was very shallow, but she was still alive. Then the sky suddenly lit up as the coast guard helicopter approached. Charlie and Alice got back into the Jeep whose engine was still running.

Once it had landed they watched as Grace was hastily transferred from the back of the ambulance and into the helicopter, she now had a drip in her arm but was still covered by the heated blankets and those that belonged to Charlie. Then as quickly as it had arrived the helicopter sped off into the night.

One of the ambulance drivers came over to Alice's window.

'They're taking her to Scarborough General, she's in hypothermia and has a shallow pulse. You need to know that it's touch and go. You did right getting her into the car asap, and we've got the warming blankets on and a drip, but it depends on how long she's been out there for.' Said the ambulance driver.

'What are her chances?' asked Alice.

'To be honest I don't know. There are three levels of hypothermia, mild, moderate and severe. At the minute your friend is classed as moderate/severe. Her pulse is very weak and she was beginning to become rigid. Hopefully you've got to her ok. Are you going over to the hospital?'

Charlie and Alice both nodded, totally in shock at the news of Grace's condition.

'Ok well take it steady if you're heading that way, there's a lot of black ice. Are you both ok, must have been a shock?'

'I wish she'd told us. What should we do about her car?' asked Charlie. 'She didn't have keys on her so they must be in the car, hang on I'll check.'

Getting out of the car she went to the driver's door of the MG and it opened and finding the jacket with keys in the pocket she waved them in the air.

'If I were you I'd move it, they charge you a lot if you don't have a ticket, could one of you drive it?'

Charlie who got back into the driver's seat of the Jeep nodded. 'We'll sort it don't worry. Thanks for the warning.'

He then went to the back of the ambulance, shut the doors and drove off into the night.

'Christ Charlie. Do you think she'll be ok?'

'I don't know love; I wish I'd known she was in such a bad way. Do you want to drive mine and I'll take Grace's? One of us needs to ring Lou as well.'

'I'll drive yours and ring Lou on the way, don't think Grace's old MG will have Bluetooth.'

'Possibly not, can you put the hospital address into the sat nav, unless you know where it is?'

Alice took Charlie's keys and gave her a kiss. 'I know where it is roughly, but will put it in the sat nav, it's been a while since I've been. I can ring Lou on the way.'

'Ok love take it slow won't you, not sure how her car will be in ice and don't want to lose you on the country roads,' said Charlie heading off to get into Grace's car.

Programming the hospital into the sat nav they set off in convoy, Alice dialled Lou's number.

'Thank god you've called, I've been so worried, did you find her?'

'We did and they've taken her off in the coastguards helicopter. It's touch and go.' Alice explained what the ambulance driver had told them.

'Oh my god, what should we do? Should we tell her parents?'

'Her parents have gone off on holiday, Grace told me they set off this morning to spend the New Year on the Orient Express. There isn't much they could do, but if it's really bad I'll find a way to get in touch with them, no point worrying them until we know more. I'm sure Grace wouldn't want us to tell them.'

'I think you're right. Do you want us to come over? If you send me the address Henry could bring me?'

'No it's ok, we'll head over there now, there isn't much anyone can do right now, they just have to bring her round and then we need to find a way to properly help her. I wish she'd talked to us.'

'Me too. Please keep us updated won't you.'

'Of course, we'll be at the hospital shortly. Will text when we know more. Love you Lou,' Alice said close to tears.

'Love to you too darling.'

The journey was slow, the roads towards Scarborough were far worse than the ones from York so they drove slowly, navigating the roads around a dark and firmly closed seaside town. They arrived at the hospital, its car park almost empty, so paying for parking for both cars they headed into the Accident and Emergency department.

'Hi, our friend Grace Star was brought in by helicopter in the last hour, can you tell us how she is please,' asked Alice.

'Let me check for you,' said the receptionist typing the name into the computer. 'Do you have her date of birth and address?'

'I don't know sorry, her address is The Annexe, Manor House, Main St, Askham Bryan. I don't know the postcode; I gave some of the details to the ambulance crew.'

'Are you related to Grace?'

'No we're her friends. Her parents are away abroad and she doesn't have any siblings. Please can you tell us how she is.'

'Ok, I'll go and find out someone to come and talk to you, could you take a seat over there please.' And with that she got up and went through some double doors.

'I'm guessing they aren't supposed to tell us are they. Maybe we should try and get in touch with her parents?'

'Let's just see what the doctors say. Should we have said she is a Dr too?'

'I don't know.'

The receptionist came back through the doors and approached them.

'The doctor will be through as soon as she can to talk to you, maybe get yourselves a drink as it might be a while.'

Alice nodded and thanked her.

'Should we call Helen?'

'No I think Helen is the last person we should call. Nothing good can come of that. She's not been good for our Grace.'

Alice nodded and going over to the vending machine got them two hot chocolates which was usually the best thing to get from them. She returned and handed one to Charlie.

Charlie gave a smile of thanks and got her phone out and began googling the symptoms of hypothermia, Alice put her head on her shoulder and read the screen too.

'Do you think we got there on time?'

'I don't know, I'm just glad that we found her, thank god for that app.'

'I know, think we should both have it, just in case.'

'Good plan, though I don't intend letting you out of my sight my love,' said Charlie.

After an hour or so a doctor came through the doors and after speaking to the receptionist she motioned for them both to follow her through the doors and down a corridor into an office.

'Sorry to keep you waiting, it's been a busy night. I understand that you're both friends of Grace's?'

'Yes we are, how is she?'

'It took us a while to stabilise her, and we are keeping a close eye on her but I think that you found her in time. She's a very lucky woman. Another ten minutes and I don't think we would be having this conversation.'

'Can we see her? Is she conscious?'

'She's not fully conscious yet, and I'd like her to rest, could you maybe come back in the morning? She'll need to speak to one of the mental health team as soon as she is able to, she will no doubt be confused and upset so maybe you could support her with that? She's in critical care at the minute and will be moved upstairs once we're sure she's ok. Maybe give us a ring in the morning and they'll tell you what ward she's on before you come in?'

'Thanks doctor, we can't thank you enough for everything that you did, we'll be back in the morning.'

They both walked out of the hospital and back to Charlie's Jeep.

'Where shall we go? I don't know any hotels here; I know there's loads of B&B's but they won't be open now.'

Alice got out her phone and googled the local hotels, finding one fairly quickly that not only had late check in but also a 24hr car park. 'Ok I've booked us in, can you bring Grace's car and we can put it there safely til we can take her home?'

Charlie nodded and so they set off to the hotel, very tired by this point and drained of emotion. Upon arrival Charlie checked them in, paid for parking for both cars and once in their room they both crashed fast asleep in minutes. A combination of the sea air and tiredness you only get on the coast.

Alice awoke a few times in the night, checking her phone each time, but there were no messages from Lou and she soon drifted off again listening to the sound of waves on the nearby beach.

They were woken at 7.30 by room service, Charlie as ever super-efficient had order it the night before. They had tea and toast and some porridge and after quick showers Alice rang the hospital. Grace had indeed been moved to a side room off the emergency care unit and was awake, so they gathered their things and headed back to the hospital. Grace had told the ward sister that she was ok with them visiting and due to the circumstances they allowed them to go in outside of visiting hours.

They easily found the ward and were directed to the side room where Grace's name was on a card outside. She looked so tired and pale laid in the bed, looking out of the window as rain suddenly started to lash down against it.

'Grace are we ok to come in?' asked Alice.

There was a faint 'yes' from the bed, she didn't turn to look at them, continuing to look out at the rain.

'We're so sorry, we'd no idea that you were feeling so bad, if we'd known……'

'I................ I just couldn't tell anyone. I feel so bad for wasting everyone's time.'

'You haven't at all. I just wish either you'd told someone or I'd realised when I saw you yesterday. We all love you, you know that don't you,' said Alice taking Grace's hand.

' You must be so disappointed in me. I'm disappointed in myself. Can you forgive me?'

'There's nothing to forgive. You were in a bad place sweetheart, so glad we found you.'

'How did you ....' she trailed off and looked out of the window again.

'The app on your phone from horse riding with Lou.'

'So Lou knows too, oh god I'm so embarrassed.'

'There's no need, we're all here for you love. We're all concerned and will do whatever it takes to help you. Do you want to talk about what happened?'

Grace shook her head. 'The mental health team will be here soon. I haven't told them I'm a doctor, did you?'

'No we didn't. Should we have?' asked Alice.

'It's ok I'll need to tell them; it'll have an impact on my job most likely. My career could be over.'

'Really?' asked Charlie.

'Yes, you don't want a suicidal doctor wielding a scalpel do you?'

'Well let's not worry about that now, what can we do? Do you want us to stay whilst you talk to the team?'

'No it's ok, but will you come back later?'

'Of course, we can stay as long as you need us, you can come and stay with us too when they discharge you if you wanted to?'

'Let's see, they might want me to stay for treatment or maybe I can go private, I really need to sort myself out.'

'We're here when you're ready to talk, anytime at all, you know that?'

'Thanks, I really appreciate it. Is my car still in Flamborough?'

'No, we've brought it here to Scarborough, it's in the hotel car park for safe keeping.'

'You really do think of everything don't you. Do you have my phone?'

'Sorry no, where is it?'

'Somewhere in my car, it's not important right now. Just don't want mum and dad worrying if they rang.'

'I'll have a look when we get back to the hotel. We'll wait there for news. Now you rest, we'll ring the ward later, we're staying at the Royal Oak up the road if you want to get hold of us.'

'Thanks, I really appreciate you both. See you later?'

'Of course. See you later,' said Charlie as they left the room and closed the door behind them.

They exited the hospital and as they got into the Jeep Charlie sighed heavily.

'Are you ok love?' asked Alice.

'I didn't tell Grace but I have her phone, it was in the pocket of her jacket with her car keys. It's full of messages from Helen. Really vile ones, well they started off nice, but I'm guessing that Grace had turned off the ringer and she'd sent a load as she drove last night. When she didn't reply the messages got vile. I can't read the whole thing but you can see the clip of it on the home screen,' she said passing the phone over to Alice.

Alice looked at the messages on the screen starting with, 'Please ring me' through to 'Stop playing games' 'How can you be so cruel to me' 'I love you' 'Stop being a bitch, you don't deserve me.'

'I think there are more but we can't see them there have been so many. I don't want Grace to see them, well not yet. She doesn't need this.'

'Does it really say I love you?'

'Yeah why?'

'Because one of the things she said yesterday was how Helen kept telling her that they weren't in a relationship, that she didn't love her even though Grace had told her. I think she got a kick out of hearing it one way. I think she wore her down to this.' Alice bowed her head. 'I'm ashamed that I didn't see this sooner.'

'None of us did, we weren't looking for it, and to be fair, she didn't say anything to anyone. Please don't feel guilty love, we found her, she's going to be ok. We need to keep her away from Helen and help her heal.'

Alice nodded. 'Can we go for a walk on the seafront, I need to be battered by the elements a bit. Just to feel grounded. I feel really sad.'

'Sure, direct me?' asked Charlie.

So as Charlie drove following Alice's directions, first to the North Bay where they stopped and had a walk on the beach where the tide was out. The wind was full on and the rain lashed down at one point. If that happened at home Alice knew they would rush for cover, but here beside the sea she relished in it and felt totally free and happy.

Once they'd been thoroughly battered they headed to South Bay and parking up on the seafront carpark they went across the road to the Harbour Bar for Horlicks served in a tall glass, just as it had been when she was a child. This time she could reach the stools without being lifted up by her dad. The café hadn't changed a bit in the 50 years she'd been going there, the staff wearing the same yellow checked uniforms and the walls adorned with advertisements for delights such as Knickerbockerglory and Banana Splits. Happy memories and a welcome shelter from the elements.

'Anything else on Grace's phone?' asked Alice taking a sip of her drink.

Charlie got out the phone and on the screen typed in capital letters was one text from Helen which read 'FUCK YOU'.

'Bloody hell, how could she write that? I thought this was a grown-up woman not a teenager having a temper tantrum,' said Charlie.

'It's uncalled for is what it is,' said Alice, her eyes flashing with anger. 'Grace had been gaslighted, you can see it just from these messages today. She's a lovely person and doesn't deserve any of this. Is there anything we can do? Should we try and tell Helen to back off?'

'I don't know how to get hold of her, I know she works at the hospital but I've no idea what her name is. Plus I don't think us getting involved in that would help in the long run. No doubt she will be nice as pie for a while if she finds out about this.'

'True. Do you think she love bombed her over summer? Do you remember all the texts?'

'I don't know, but it was bloody full on from the get go.'

'I only know from what one of my students was telling me during a supervision, a boyfriend who basically did all that kind of stuff, texting, calling and wanting to know where she was all the time. Telling her what she wanted to hear to a point, then pulling away, totally push and pull. The poor lass didn't know if she was coming or going. She had to block him and everything for it to stop. Took months.'

'God what's happened to dating? Don't people go out and have fun if that's all they're after, or get serious if that's their bag too? Why all the game playing?'

'Er.'

'I know me saying that sounds odd now, but I was always clear at the beginning that I didn't want a relationship, I was happy to have fun and go out and fool about a bit, but I never intentionally led anyone on. I was always upfront.'

'Maybe they just had crossed wires?'

'Maybe,' replied Charlie. 'Do you think I was like Helen?'

'God no, not at all, this seems deliberate, I just hope that Grace can tell us what has really gone on one day. We can help her then.'

'True. Think I'll give the hospital a call, see what's happening, you finish off your drink,' said Charlie, standing and heading out of the café. She felt a rush of sadness that maybe the women she'd dallied with had felt like Grace too. The woman from the Todmorden disco had certainly had her say on what a bitch she had been to her.

Dialling the hospital she got through to the switchboard who transferred her to the ward. After a few minutes she was put through to the ward clerk who said that Grace was being discharged just after lunchtime, and were they going to collect her?

Going back into the Harbour Bar Charlie relayed what the hospital had said so finishing off their drinks they headed back to the Jeep and headed to pick up Grace. Alice texted Lou to let her know what was happening and by the time they arrived at the carpark it was almost one o'clock.

Carrying the clothes that Grace had left in her car they went up to the ward. Grace was sat in the chair, still wearing a hospital gown.

'We brought these from your car in case you wanted to change?'

'Thanks,' said Grace reaching out and taking them.

'What did the doctor say? What do you want to do?' asked Alice.

'I've made an appointment with a private therapist, there aren't many NHS options and I can't wait around for that. My local mental health team will be in touch but in the meantime they said I could go home.'

'Is that what you want to do? You're more than welcome to come and stay with us.' Charlie knew that she needed to talk to her about the texts before she gave the phone back, especially if she was alone.

'I don't know what I need to be honest. Could I maybe stay tonight and see how I am tomorrow?'

'No worries, play it by ear. When are you seeing a therapist?'

'Tomorrow is my first session, she's only in Acomb so not far to go. Not sure I'm up for driving back though, would you mind if I one of you drove mine back?'

'Not a problem. You go with Alice in the Jeep and I'll follow in yours. Shall we go to the annexe and get you some clothes? I'm sure Lou would love to see you too.'

Grace welled up. 'You're all so kind, I don't deserve this. I feel such a let-down.'

'We're your friends and we're here to help. Now you get dressed and we can get you back. We're all happy to do this. You're our pal,' said Charlie. Not used to sentimental words to friends she shuffled her feet and looked off into the distance as though it was the most interesting thing to see.

After thanking the staff Grace took her paperwork and they headed back to the car. After picking up the MG they all headed back to York. Charlie was very tempted to open up the MG and really give it a good blast, but she refrained. It was a lovely car and she felt like a racing driver compared to driving the Jeep.

Lou and Henry were out when they got back to the annexe so Grace gathered some clothes and toiletries and they went back to Alice's house.

Once they got her settled in the spare room and showed her how everything worked Charlie went down to the kitchen whilst Alice helped her unpack.

Charlie had a quick look in the fridge and put some sausages in the oven, peeled some potatoes and opened a tin of beans. This really did call for comfort food. Just before it was ready Alice and Grace came downstairs and they ate in semi silence in the dining room. Grace didn't eat much but moved the food around her plate.

'Can I get you something else? Tea or coffee?'

'A coffee would be good, I only had one at the hospital and I need more caffeine. I'm so tired.

'You've been through a lot, you go through to the living room and I'll bring the coffee through,' said Alice, as Charlie cleared the table.

Looking in the cupboard she found some Christmas cake and a cheese board in the fridge and some crackers, so making up a tray she took it through.

Grace took a mug of black coffee and added some sugar to it, then curling up in the corner chair she held it with both hands as though still frozen from the night before.

Charlie, ever the hostess handed her a piece of cake with cheese on top which she nibbled at in small pieces, leaving the icing with marzipan until last, like you do when you were a kid.

'Thanks, I do appreciate this.'

'You don't need to thank us, it's all ok Grace.'

'Do you think I should contact my mum and dad? They'll be on the train by now I think.'

'It's up to you, do you want them to come home?' asked Alice finishing off her coffee and cake.

'I don't know, it's almost instinctual to want your parents isn't it.'

Both Alice and Charlie, who hadn't had good relationships with their parents didn't comment.

Grace continued. 'But I don't want to spoil their holiday, I'm ok, I'm safe here, but I feel so lost.'

'Do you want to talk about what happened? What made you want to do what you did?'

'That's what the mental health team asked me too. It's been so many things. I'm so tired with work, worrying about my job, not knowing what end is up most days. Things that wouldn't normally affect me massively really have started eating away at me. Then Helen. I don't know what I'm doing wrong. Everything I say or do upsets her. We'll be alright for a week or so then end up fighting, or should I say she will walk out, or hang up or say such awful things. I don't know what to do.'

'It sounds very confusing,' said Alice gently.

Grace nodded. 'Did you find my phone in the car?' she asked Charlie.

Charlie looked over at Alice who nodded discreetly.

'It was in your coat pocket with your keys. We haven't looked properly but there were a lot of messages last night and today from Helen. They aren't nice Grace. She shouldn't be messaging you stuff like that. I'm not sure you should look at them. Do you want me to delete them?'

Grace lowered her eyes looking into the wood burner. 'I don't know. I don't think I can take anymore.'

'Well maybe just leave it for now.'

'I do need to check and see if my parents have messaged, if I don't reply they'll worry.'

'Do you want me to hide the messages from her, so the messages don't come through?' asked Charlie.

Grace nodded so Charlie swiped away the messages on the home screen from Helen, then handed the phone over to Grace who opened the phone with facial recognition. Then Charlie archived the messages, there were 15 of them on Whatsapp so that they could be looked at later but not in Grace's face.

'There you go, I've put them in archive for now. If she messages it won't ping.'

'Thanks.' Grace looked at her other messages and replied to one from her parents to say they were boarding the Orient Express sent the night before. She handed the phone back to Charlie. 'Can you keep it; I don't want to be tempted to look at it.'

'Sure, I'll put it on charge in the office later. Can I get you anything?'

'No I'm just very tired, I think I'll go up and have a rest if that's ok?' said Grace standing up slowly.

'Now that sounds like a plan, let me help you upstairs, I'll just be next door if you need me. You don't mind if I desert you and have a nap too do you?' asked Alice.

'Not at all my love, have a nice rest,' said Charlie putting her feet up on the coffee table, holding the remote. 'I'll find a nice Christmas movie.'

Alice smiled, she knew that within 10 minutes Charlie would be fast asleep on the sofa with Bing Crosby singing his heart out to White Christmas, they'd already watched it twice in the past week.

So the two friends headed upstairs and once Grace was settled Alice headed for a lie down too, the last few days had really knocked the stuffing out of her.

Chapter Twenty-Five – Was it really I love you?

The gap between Christmas and New Year always tends to drag where you don't know what day of the week it is. The goal is to make it intact to New Years Eve, raise a toast at midnight, then slide on into the brand-new year with new possibilities.

Alice had always hated New Year's Eve. As a kid she was dragged to grown up events where strangers would kiss you at midnight, it felt invasive and inappropriate, but that was the 1970's where women put up and shut up. Nowadays all she wanted to do was curl up with Charlie on the sofa, watch the fireworks from London on the television and then go to bed together. That's what they'd done last year and it'd been such a peaceful and calm way to start afresh. This year however they'd been invited to Lou and Henry's. A final hurrah for his 60th birthday, it had been such a massive year for them so they felt they couldn't say no. Grace had stayed with them since being discharged from hospital, she wasn't in the right frame of mind to be part of the celebrations but equally didn't want to be alone either. So a couple of hours before the party was due to start they headed to her annexe next door to Lou's so she could get ready but also have a place to escape to if the need arose.

After parking they went through the gate and at her front door was a wilting bunch of flowers, a card sticking out of the side.

'Can you open it, I don't want to look,' said Grace putting the key in the lock and stepping over the flowers.

Charlie picked up the card, opened it and sure enough they were from Helen. The card read.

Please forgive me, I'm sorry. Ring me. Love Helen xxx

'Do you want to know what it says?' asked Charlie putting the card back in the envelope.

'Please.'

Charlie passed the envelope over to her. Taking it out she laughed out loud.

'So now she says I love you. Do you think she means it?'

'No Grace, I think it's just another game, a way to hook you back in.'

'Really? You think she'd do that?'

'It's what she's done all along, drip fed you just enough to keep you there. Please lovely, don't fall for it again.'

Grace replaced the card and ripped it into small pieces. 'Can you put the flowers in the bin. They're as dead as I feel.'

Alice took the flowers from Charlie and took them to the wheelie bin at the side of the house. As she did so she saw Lou coming up the lane.

'I thought I heard your car. How's Grace doing?' she asked.

'Better than she was, come in and say hi, she'd love to see you I'm sure.'

Entering the annexe Charlie was sitting on the sofa and swiftly put something into her inside her jacket pocket.

'Can I get you a drink? Grace has just gone in the shower.'

'No thanks. I don't know why but I feel totally queasy about tonight. Henry's been amazing and I've been zero help. I think I'll book myself into a health spa in the new year, even Henry has slowed down on the cooking.'

Alice nodded vigorously. 'I totally get you, salads all round until Easter.'

'I wouldn't go that far,' smiled Lou. 'But I need to go on a diet, none of my skirts fit me.'

'I feel you,' said Charlie. I'm thinking of elasticated trousers are the way forward.'

They laughed.

'Anyway I better get back, I just needed to take a breather. See you in a while, give my love to Grace, tell her it's ok if she doesn't want to stay for the whole party but it'd be lovely to see her.'

'We'll tell her, see you soon.'

Lou closed the door behind her and Alice joined Charlie on the sofa.

'What's that smile for? What are you plotting? I know that look.'

'Ok, you know me too well. I can't keep it a secret any longer. I wanted to tell you later but I have to tell you. Please don't get mad and if you really hate the idea then I'll drop it, but you know that farm where your grandad worked, the one that's for sale?'

'Yes,' said Alice tentatively.

'Well I put an offer in on it and today they accepted. I want to buy it for us love. A place we can make our own, it's a wreck but I think it'd be amazing.'

'Really, you're buying it for us? I don't have that sort of money Charlie.'

'I know, that's why I'm buying it for us. The money isn't important, us making it our home is what matters to me. Do you hate the idea?'

'I don't even know what it looks like.'

Charlie brought out some papers from her inside pocket and handed them to Alice.

Alice unfolded the property details of Ashfield Farm and read them intently, page by page.

'What would we do with it? It's gorgeous Charlie, and the house is amazing, but what could we do with the outbuildings?'

'I've been researching wedding venues for us, some are too much, others are not enough, none seem just what we want, somewhere small and intimate but full of love. I think this is it Alice, I think this is the place I want us to get married, where others could do it too.'

Alice looked back at the details.

'Oh god are you mad at me? Have I over stepped?'

'I can't deny it's a shock, and I'm not sure how I feel about the amount of money you will have to spend on it, but I love the wedding idea. Can we go and see it?'

'Of course, I've got the owners number, she said to call anytime. Shall I see if we can go tomorrow or do you need more time to think?'

'No I think I want to see it as soon as I can. It looks amazing, but can you afford it?'

'I've been selling my assets, the pubs and houses I own, it's more than enough. When I sell my house that'll pay for the renovations.'

'But what about my contribution? When I sell my house I could invest in it too.'

'No love. I want you to keep your house, I never want you to feel like you have nowhere to go if anything went wrong between us. I want to buy the farm for us, make it our home.'

'I'm not sure how I feel about that, it'd be like being a kept woman.'

'Would it? I'm sorry I don't want you to think that.'

'Well let's go and look at it and then talk some more, it's an amazing idea love,' she said giving her a big hug.

Grace, fresh from the shower came out of her room in a white fluffy dressing gown.

'Shall I make you some tea?' asked Charlie.

'That'd be lovely, do you think you could take those things and put them in your car until I decide what to do with them?' she said pointing to the presents earmarked for Helen's Christmas presents and all of her things that she had refused to take with her.

'Of course, anything else you want me to remove?'

'No that's all I think. Can you check the post box for me as well? The key's on the hook,' she said pointing to where it lived on the kitchen wall.

Alice collected a small mountain of post, some delayed Christmas cards, brown envelopes with windows and a small box with a printed label. Handing them to Grace she immediately opened the box which contained a sim card.

'I decided the easiest way to stop Helen contacting me was to change my number so I've got a new sim card. Can you help me transfer everything?'

'Don't look at me,' said Alice. 'I'm not that technical. Charlie's your woman.'

'I didn't bring the phone with me, it's still at Alice's, am I ok to do it later? Will need to back up your contacts and stuff.'

'Yes that's fine, as long as she can't contact me again. I'm determined I won't let her back in. I promise.'

'You don't have to do that for us, we want to see you happy, we just don't think she can. I don't know what's wrong with the woman but she's been so horrible to you, I wish we'd known how bad it'd got.'

'I didn't want anyone to know, I honestly thought it was me, that I was the problem, I can't believe how low I got. I need to talk to my manager and see where I go from here, if Helen goes through with her threat I'll lose my job, it'd be the end of my career I've worked so hard for. The shame it'd bring on my parents, on me. I couldn't bear it.'

'Personally I think it's an empty threat, she would be making an idiot of herself because I'm sure you're very well thought of. We don't know her, nor her background. Do you know how long she's been working at your hospital, don't think you said how long you've known her?'

'She hasn't worked there long at all, think she came last year. She was near Leicester before she came to York I believe.'

'Well who's to say that she hasn't done this before elsewhere. It could be a pattern, but I agree you should talk to your manager pronto.'

'I will. Now I better go get dressed so we can get to Lou's. Am I ok to stay with you for a few more days?'

'Of course, stay as long as you want to,' said Charlie knowing that Alice would agree.

'Thanks, I'll pack a bag and put it in your car on the way out, I appreciate everything you've done for me, I really do.'

'We don't want thanks; we just want you to be happy.'

Grace hugged them both then went to get dressed.

'I'm glad she wants to come back with us, such a relief actually,' said Charlie.

'Me too, it's been a hell of a few days, I hope next year is calmer,' replied Alice.

'Do you think the farm and wedding thing is too much of a stretch? Too much for us?'

'No, I just don't know what I can bring to the table?'

'You'll bring your style to the house, your input into the wedding things, you could have a horse again……'

'You'd do all of that for me?' Alice said welling up.

'I'd do anything for you, anything at all.'

'Oh Charlie. God I love you, I feel so lucky,' Alice snuggled up close, wrapped up in her lovers arms and there they sat for some time, just immersed in each other until Grace came out of her bedroom with a holdall with her things in.

'All sorted, ready when you are,' said Grace. 'Can I put it in your car now, saves coming back again?'

'Sure,' said Charlie getting her keys out of her pocket.

'I need to check on my parents' house, move post and stuff, do you want to have a look? I know how you both like your house spotting.'

'Thought you'd never ask, always wondered what it's like inside,' Alice replied smiling, she remembered riding past the house so often growing up so she was intrigued to what if the house matched the fantasy she'd imagined.

So after putting the bag in the car they had a brief tour of the house, Charlie deep in thought, Alice admiring the original features and swooning over the Aga.

'Mum and dad want me to take over the house, it seem such a waste just me living in it. I'm not sure what to do. So if either of you have any bright ideas?'

'Funny you should say that' said Charlie. 'I've an idea about starting up a wedding venue near here, what about if your house was let out for the bridal party, or at least part of it? Honeymoon suite and stuff like that, it feels so elegant and homely.'

'That's an interesting idea, I like the idea of the wedding venue too. I couldn't accommodate many though.'

'It wouldn't need to, I'm thinking small intimate weddings, more personal. Not having to invite a million relatives if you didn't want to.'

Grace laughed. 'Now that sounds a brilliant plan. Well let's think about it more and come up with something maybe. It sounds fun actually.'

Alice smiled, she admired how Charlie's brain worked, not just as a businesswoman but also as a friend. Knowing it would give Grace something positive to think of, to hopefully take her away from the dark place she'd gone to.

'Right we better get to the party. We'll be the fashionably late ones.'

The trio walked down the lane to Lou and Henry's, the patio doors were open despite the weather, that could only mean one thing, Henry had been cooking again and the kitchen was a hot spot.

The kitchen was heaving as they entered, many people they'd never met, some they recognised from the birthday party, and in the corner were Jen, Holly and Harriet, all of whom were howling with laughter.

Walking over to join them Lou and Henry emerged from the hallway and greeted them.

'Drinks are over there when you're ready, food is a buffet all laid out in the dining room, chairs are at a premium so you might have to elbow your way in,' said Henry.

'How are you doing? Feeling better?' Alice asked Lou.

'Not really, I still feel quite queasy. Think I'll pay a visit to the doc next week, though she'll probably say it's overindulging over Christmas.'

'It can't help to check, but how long have you felt like this?' asked Holly.

'Quite a few weeks, in fact it's almost a month actually, it was before Henry's party, I put it down to the stress of organising it. God you don't think it's serious do you?'

'No not at all, I'm sure it's just all the food, we're all feeling a bit bloated, plus the stress of your breast cancer scare, it's been a hell of a lot to deal with.'

'Can I get anyone a drink?' asked Jen, I'm just going for a top up.'

'We'll come with you,' said Alice, so they went in the direction of the drinks area in the kitchen leaving Lou and Holly talking. Grace spotted a couple of her other neighbours and went over to chat to them.

After selecting a drink they headed to look for the food headed by Jen who as ever was keen as mustard to see what was on offer. She piled up a plate from the beige buffet on one side of the dining room, leaving the technicolour array of salads on the other side alone.

'Come on sis, think healthy thoughts,' said Charlie laughing.

'Plenty of time for that yet, New Year isn't for another 3 hours, still time left to be bad before that.'

'Health kick starts tomorrow eh?'

'Yeah Holly is making me join a gym, can you imagine it!'

'Not really no,' laughed Alice. 'I can't see you head to toe in Lycra.'

'Oh god I hadn't thought of that. You don't think she'll make me wear Lycra?'

'She might,' said Charlie smirking. 'Feel the burn and all that.'

'For fuck sake,' replied Jen piling more sausage rolls on her plate. 'Better make the most of it then hadn't I.'

They went back through to the kitchen; Lou was nowhere to be seen and Holly was refreshing her drink.

'Brought you some grub lass, lots of salad for you,' Jen said handing over a plate with a fork and a lot of greenery, a solitary slice of pork pie sat on top of the mound.'

'I can't see any greenery on your plate Jen,' laughed Holly. 'Health kick starts tomorrow has she told you?'

'Yeah she did, it's hilarious, matching Lycra outfits and all that lesbian stuff?'

'Lesbian stuff?'

'Yeah it's a thing, lesbians exercising on TikTok, you'll have to start your own page, become influencers of a certain age.'

'We're in our prime, look at these muscles,' said Jen flexing.

'Impressive sis, you'll definitely have to film it, even if it's only just for us,' laughed Charlie.

'It's not a bad idea joining the gym,' said Alice. 'Maybe we could all go together.'

'Now I don't think.......' started Charlie.

'It'd be loads of fun, the four of us, we could have a competition who can run fastest or furthest without needing an ambulance.'

Alice was in stitches looking at Charlie's face, she had wound her up good and proper.

'Ooo you minx, I honestly thought you were serious. Just wait until I get you home.'

'Promises, promises,' squealed Alice as Charlie pinched her bum.

'Get a room,' said Jen.

'Excuse me a minute,' said Holly going off in the direction of Lou who had beckoned her over, then after a few words were passed between them they went off down the hallway together.

'I hope Lou is ok, she's been looking peaky. Hopefully once tonight is over she can have a proper rest,' said Alice.

They all looked down the hallway, Holly returned and went and talked to Henry who followed her back to where Lou was stood. Unable to stop herself Alice followed.

'Sorry but is everything ok?'

'Do you want to do this alone Lou? We can always go back to the party,' said Holly joining Alice's side.

'No, but let's go do this upstairs if that's ok. I need to sit down.'

The four of them headed upstairs to Lou and Henry's room where a white carved four poster bed stood, a sofa in the bay window and the creamiest carpets Alice had ever seen.

After sitting, Henry joined her, his face full of concern.

'What is it? Is it bad Holly, do we need an ambulance?'

Holly gave Alice a brief smile then turned and looked calmly at Lou who was very pale.

'Henry, this is going to be a bit of a shock and I'm not quite sure how to tell you, but ……'

'Oh god,' he said running his hands nervously through his hair. 'Please tell me. God haven't we been through enough this year.'

'Henry my darling,' she said taking his hands in hers. 'I'm pregnant. I don't know how or why it's happened after all of these years but I'm pregnant. I told Holly how unwell I've felt and a few other things that I hadn't mentioned like sore boobs, but I put that down to the prodding and poking at the hospital. Anyway Holly had a test in her doctors bag and I've just taken it. And I'm pregnant. We're going to have a baby Henry. After all these years we're going to have a baby.'

Henry sat there; his mouth wide open. He looked at Holly. 'Is it accurate, could it be a mistake?'

'I don't think so. I think Lou needs to see her doctor ASAP but yes she's pregnant. There are high risks because of her age, sorry love,' Holly said looking at a joyful Lou. 'But if we look after her really well, then yes she'll be having a baby in about six months' time I think. Because of the perimenopause and periods being all over it's hard to know without a scan, but I'm so very happy for you both.

Alice stood, tears streaming down her face. 'It might be too early for congratulations, but I am so very happy for you both. Such amazing news.'

'I don't want anyone to know downstairs, until we know everything, but it's ok to tell Jen and Charlie as it'll be hard not to say anything, well for you Alice, Holly will be used to keeping secrets. But as soon as we know for definite I want to tell the whole world. Oh my god Henry.'

They sat there hugging and crying and so Alice and Holly left them alone to come to terms with their news.

At the top of the stairs Alice asked, 'It's risky isn't it, with being over 50.'

Holly nodded, 'Let's see what the next few weeks brings. It might all be ok.'

They both headed back downstairs to rejoin the party, trying very hard to compose themselves before facing everyone. Charlie raised her eyebrows in the 'is everything ok' way. Alice gave her a nod. Jen however was lost in party mode, entertaining some of Henry's London friends. The party went on and on. Somewhere someone put on some music and people began to relax thanks to the flowing wine. Lou and Henry returned and danced in the kitchen cheek to cheek to 'Lady in Red' and other 80's classics. It was like they wanted to stay as close together as they could and not have to interact with people. The night wore on and it was soon midnight.

Henry tapped his glass with a teaspoon to gain everyone's attention, someone put on the radio where the peels of Big Ben could be heard and the countdown to midnight drew near. The crowd counted, and at the toll of midnight they all cheered Happy New Year. Someone popped some corks; champagne was passed around, and everyone grabbed the person nearest them to kiss. Grace had made a swift exit before the bells rang, and Alice noticed that Lou hadn't taken any champagne when offered, instead she had poured a glass of orange juice in readiness.

After Auld Lang Syne had been sung and more hugs all round people began to say their goodnights. Lou and Henry looked shattered so they all bid goodnight and headed home in their respective cars or walked home. Holly drove a rather tipsy Jen home, Grace decided to stay with them overnight to give a break to Alice and Charlie who headed back to York. She hadn't told Charlie Lou's news yet; she didn't want to blurt it out in front of Grace and she wasn't sure whether to wait until they knew more. It had certainly been quite a night, Charlie had given her so much to think about, the possibilities of an amazing future with her lovely fiancée. Now that was indeed something lovely to go to sleep on.

Chapter Twenty-Six – To build the future

The following morning, bright eyed and bushy tailed Charlie checked her phone. She'd texted the seller of Ashfield Farm the previous night to ask when she could view again. She really wanted Alice to see the farm whilst the thought was in their heads. There was a reply that they'd be welcome to come over that day if they wanted and to just let her know what time.

Smiling she rolled over and watched a sleeping Alice. The thin sheet only drawn up to her waist, her breasts open to the coldness of the room her perfect nipples pert and inviting. Charlie resisted for now.

Running her fingers gently down the side of Alice's face she slowly began to wake, her blonde hair cascading across the pillow. Opening her blue eyes she looked up at Charlie who was on her side, resting her head on her right hand, her left hand gently drawing circles across Alice's body.

Nuzzling closer into Charlie, Alice reached up for a kiss, the softest, morning kiss, filled with dreams just gone and the present beautifulness of their love. Continuing to circle her fingers she traced a perfect arc around Alice's nipple, moving slowly into the centre to tweak the perfect receptive nipple. Letting out a loud moan Alice gripped Charlie's thigh.

Breaking away from kissing Alice suddenly looked desperate, a look that Charlie longed to see, she knew exactly what she needed. Today was not a day of long lingering touches, today she needed to come, and come fast.

Charlie was always happy to oblige as she loved to see her come and to see her writhe with pleasure. To give in to the deep longing she had.

'Do you want it hard or soft, left or right?'

'Your right hand and hard. Please Charlie, make me come hard.'

'Maybe. Maybe I want to take my time.'

She could see the desperate look in her eye.

'Spread your legs,' she commanded.

Alice obliged.

'Wider. Now!'

She did as she was told.

Charlie fingers, quickly spread her wide open, sliding one finger into her slowly. 'More,' she begged.

'No, wait, not too fast.'

'I want it, I want it now,' Alice pleaded.

She was wiggling around trying to place herself correctly onto Charlie's palm.

'Cheeky, you really do want it don't you.'

'Please!'

Charlie really wanted to make her wait, see how long she could keep her on edge but she also wanted to see her come, a sight that was stunning to witness. She'd never seen a woman enjoy sex as much as Alice, that in itself was a massive turn on.

Thrusting two fingers deep as she could, curling them around she slowly built up the pressure on her G spot, her thumb soft on her clit she let her ride her fingers up and down, becoming wetter and wetter until she let out a giant shudder, her hand gripping the bed on one side, Charlie's thigh the other. Onwards she exploded over and over, the moans getting louder, her breath so fast until she screamed out, grasping her thigh so hard she shrieked herself. Slowly she stopped, Alice contorted rigid on the bed whispering 'oh my god' repeatedly.

Charlie reached down and kissed her softly, she unfurled and cuddled into Charlie's chest.

'Wow where did that come from?'

'I was dreaming about you; it was like the dream continued. That was so hot.'

'What was I doing to you in your dream?'

'We were at the farm, the one we want to buy.'

'We want to buy. Are you really thinking about it?'

'Of course, I haven't thought of much else. Can we go and see it soon?'

'Actually the owner texted, we could go today if you wanted? Or do you need more time?'

'Not at all, I really want to see it, today would be great, whenever suits them really.'

'Brill, I'll message her now. Sure you don't mind?'

'Other than making love to you I can't think of anything I'd like to do more.'

'Well let me text her now and then you can do that with my absolute pleasure.'

Alice smiled as she began kissing Charlie as she slowly made her way down exploring with her tongue.

'God woman, I can't spell when you do that. Oh my god Alice, you bad, bad woman.'

'My pleasure.'

'No I think you'll find it's mine.'

A couple of hours later, freshly showered and dressed they were making their way to Ashfield Farm. It was a beautiful but cold winters day so they were wrapped up warm, well until a hot flush kicked in that is.

Mrs Bland was waiting for them as they pulled in front of the house. Alice's face was beaming.

'Oh Charlie, it's nicer than the brochure by a million miles.'

'Let's try and play it cool, don't want them ramping up the price because we love it,' laughed Charlie.

'Ok boss, I'll be good.'

The owner greeted them and began by showing them the farmyard and outbuildings. Alice was trying desperately not to see her very own project with these Victorian buildings, it was perfect. Plus thinking about her grandad working there too. How wonderful it would be to buy part of her own family history, the possibilities seemed endless. The fields were perfect too, she could imagine riding and schooling on the flat paddock to the right and grazing to the left. To wake up to those views every single day.

They all donned PPE and looked at the kitchen area, Charlie looked thoroughly around this time and Alice could tell she was doing calculations in her head.

Finishing off Mrs Bland showed them the house, Alice's eyes were sparkling as they walked around looking at all the original features, the place where an Aga would go, the fireplaces to refurbish. Yes this was a big project but it would make them an amazing home, one where they could both put down roots, be their own family.

After the tour Charlie asked a couple of questions about how long the move in process would be with there being an established business there already and finding the answer agreeable a smile spread across her face.

Alice raised her eyebrows, so much for not showing an interest. Charlie smiled sheepishly as they walked hand in hand back to the Jeep.

'Mrs Bland has said we could have another walk around outside if we wanted to? Take our time.'

'Can we just sit for a minute. Do you think we can do it? Wouldn't it cost too much money?'

'All's sorted with the money, my house is worth 500k which is more than enough for the conversions. We can do this.'

'Ok let's go look at the outbuildings again, tell me how you see them.'

So walking back into the barns Charlie gave Alice her vision of how they would refurbish them for weddings, the area for the ceremony, the meal afterwards, an area for dancing, all intimate, a maximum of 50 guests. Keeping it rustic but with a hint of glamour with the lighting and accessories, but nothing that would take away from the beauty of the buildings. All the food could be served on site, and if Grace could be persuaded they could use her house for the bridal party, and the grooms could use part of Harriet's new farm too maybe. Henry wanted to be on board too with catering in some way as well.

'What do you think? Is it too mad an idea?'

'No I think it's perfect but I want to throw my money in too, that's my part of agreeing to the deal.'

'We can work all that out love, but this will be our forever home. Forever and Always.'

Charlie took out her phone and put on Spotify and looking deep into Alice's eyes, pulled her close as the beautiful voice of Mariah Counts came out of her speaker, and just like their first date she sang to her as they danced to their favourite song.

>Can you tell me
>Have you found someone,
>Someone who loves you for yourself
>For yourself.
>Cause I think that
>I found the one
>The one who makes me kiss and tell
>Kiss and tell
>Now that I'm their biggest fan
>I let them ruin all my plans
>All my plans
>Yea, I know I've found someone,
>Someone who loves me for myself
>For myself
>Hit me am I dreaming
>Cause I'm feeling
>Like the world is on my side
>I know she got me fiending

Got me tongue tied
Tongue tied
Take what you want
Take it all from me
Take everything I own
Cause now I know
She's everything I need
(copywrite Mariah Counts 2022)

As the music faded, Alice kissed her.

'You're such a softie, I love you Charlie.'

'I love you too Alice. This is just the beginning of something really special, I can feel it in my bones.'

Alice smiled. 'I think so too, let's do this.'

Chapter Twenty-Seven– When the end has a beginning

As soon as Grace knew her boss was back at work after Christmas she arranged a meeting with her. They had worked together for over ten years so there was a level of trust that had been earned, and Grace knew she could tell her everything that had happened.

Walking into the department she received so many welcome back hugs and handshakes, people were genuinely pleased to see her. They didn't know what had happened over Christmas, no one other than her very close friends knew that, as far as they were aware she had been off sick with a virus. They all wanted to know when she would be back and she gave vague replies as she slowly made her way to the manager's office.

Knocking at the door she heard a voice telling her to enter.

'Lovely to see you Grace, take a seat,' her manager said gesturing to the chair opposite her desk. 'How are you feeling?'

'Better than I was. I needed to come in and tell you in person rather than you find out some other way. I'm just sorry I wasn't open with you earlier.'

Her manager frowned. 'Are you leaving Grace, have you come to hand in your notice?'

'No, but you may not want me back when I tell you what's happened.'

'Ok, take your time telling me. Can I get you a drink?'

'A cup of coffee would be nice thank you.'

Her manager picked up her phone and dialling her secretary requested two cups of coffee which arrived in super-fast time as her assistant knew she'd be requesting them; she knew how her boss liked her coffee, as did Grace.

Once they were settled with cups in hand Grace began to tell her what had gone on.

'Do you remember me telling you that I'd met someone last summer and we started seeing each other?'

'Yes I do, Helen from the theatre?'

Grace nodded; her eyes cast down as she continued.

'It all started well, I thought things were good between us, but she'd go off in weird moods. Ignored me for days on end for no reason, lost her temper, then would be nice as pie the next. Well it got worse and she became really angry and would make me doubt myself, I felt so unwell, I couldn't sleep. I couldn't eat, I lost my love of my job because I felt I wasn't giving it 100% and I always have done.'

'You've always been an asset to the department Grace, you know that.'

'Thank you, I really do appreciate you saying that,' said Grace taking in a large lung full of air before she continued. 'I got so depressed, I couldn't function, that's when I went off sick, I didn't want to jeopardise my patients. I'm so sorry if it's caused you or them problems.'

'We've managed, I knew something wasn't right, I just wasn't sure if I should approach you, I didn't want to put pressure on you.'

'You couldn't put more pressure on me than I was doing to myself already. Anyway around time Christmas it all got really bad. The threats, the gaslighting and then she said that she was going to ruin my career because I wasn't doing what she wanted anymore. I sank really low with depression, I couldn't think straight and I tried to end my life. If it hadn't been for my friends looking for me I wouldn't be here now. So I had to come and tell you today, before she's had a chance to start her character assassination.'

Her manager was silent for some time. 'I'm so very sorry Grace, I'd no idea it had got so bad. Is there anything I can do to help? How are you feeling now?'

'Much better than I was, shell shocked if anything, it all feels so surreal. I've had to change my phone number as she's messaged none stop. I hardly dare ask. Has she contacted you?'

'Yes I've had a letter from Helen where she'd laid out her thoughts of you and your work and general vile comments that I won't repeat. However something else has happened in the meantime.'

Grace visibly tensed in the chair. 'What's happened, I really dread to think.'

'You'll remember a patient of yours from a few months ago Juliette Smith?'

'Yes I do,' said Grace nervously, god what had Helen said about that? She didn't even really know her when that happened. She'd told her of course when talking about work things, they both had, but she was confused what else there was to add.

'You asked the staff in A&E if anyone had been with her when she was admitted.'

'Yes I remember, her mother asked me to find out, but no one had any memory of who brought her in as she wasn't brought in by ambulance it transpired.'

'Well one of the receptionists has been in touch, she'd gone on maternity leave a day after Juliette came into the department so she sadly wasn't contacted, however she had lunch with a colleague recently and they had a discussion about what happened that day.'

'Was there someone with her? I don't understand where Helen comes into all this, we weren't even together then.'

'No you weren't. However Helen was Juliette's partner, she brought her to the department when she was having her heart attack and then left her on a seat inside and then fled. The receptionist is the only one who saw her, she was in and out in a flash and she knew who Helen was from when she'd been down to consult on cases sometimes.'

'What do you mean Helen was Juliette's partner? I don't understand. How do you know?'

'Juliette's mother contacted us; she told us she'd accessed the mobile phone and it was all in there. Lots of love, care and attention in the beginning, hurtful and abusive at the end. Juliette had a heart attack and she dumped her at the hospital and left. She did the same to her that she has done to you. We are all stunned and can't believe that someone could do that once never mind twice. I'm so sorry that happened to you.'

'So Helen wore Juliette down too? Potentially made her ill?'

'Sadly so. She was a confident, successful businesswoman, then she met Helen and she became depressed, withdrew from her friends and family and it made her really unwell. Her mum doesn't know when she became ill as Helen made sure that she didn't see her. You couldn't make it up, you read about this stuff, but in real life, it's so hard to imagine.'

'I used to think the same thing. Now it's just a nightmare.'

'Let me reassure you on something, you won't be seeing Helen around. She handed in her notice, along with the letter about you. She never took holidays so she's basically off now.'

'You want me to stay? After all this?'

'You've done nothing wrong professionally, you went off sick when you knew you weren't coping, you put your patients' needs above yours for so long. I don't want you back until you're ready though. You have been through such a lot. Are you seeing a therapist?'

'Yes, my friend Holly put me in touch with someone. It's really knocked the stuffing out of me.'

'Take as long as you need and remember you can contact me anytime, I wish you'd told me sooner, but I understand why you didn't. Work will be here when you're ready to come back, just take your time.'

'I don't know how to thank you; I thought you'd want rid of me.'

'I want you to come back when you're ready, but I do want you to go away somewhere, just to get better and come back when you feel you can. With no pressure from me or the department.'

'Thank you for being so understanding. I promise to keep in touch. I feel so exhausted and no where near ready to coming back. But I will be in touch soon I promise. I just didn't want my career to end like this.'

'And it isn't over. You just need to take some time out to recover. Your job is safe, so go get some rest okay?'

Grace nodded. 'Ok I promise but I'll get going as know you're really busy. Thanks again and for the coffee.'

They said their goodbyes and Grace let out a big sigh of relief.

It took time to leave the hospital, staff wanted to chat and patients asked a ton of questions which she wasn't able to answer. It felt good to just feel normal but she felt stunned at what she'd just learnt.

Walking back to her car she dialled Alice; she and Charlie didn't live far away and she wanted to download and let them know what she'd just learnt. They were on their way home so they agreed to meet back at Alice's.

Charlie opened the door when she got there, the coffee was already made and a tin of Christmas themed biscuits were on the table. Alice's laptop was open on her knee with her legs up on the sofa.

Putting her work down on the table Alice stood up and gave Grace a hug.

'Sit down, can I pour you some coffee?' she asked.

'Absolutely, you look busy there, what are you working on now?'

Alice told her the story so far of Eliza and Gertrude, how she'd traced them from York where they were born, to the workhouse and then to a mill near Harrogate.

'Another book in the making maybe?'

Alice blushed, 'Maybe, who knows at the minute, it's a sad story though so not sure. Anyway forget about me, how are you doing Grace? How did it go at work?'

'You won't believe it when I tell you what's happened,' she said taking a sip of coffee.

Grace related what her manager had told her. That Helen had been in a relationship with Juliette, that she'd done the same to her too. That it wasn't her fault. It was what she does, took pleasure in it too probably.

'What a bitch,' said Alice. 'I'm stunned, it was bad enough that she did it to you, but the fact she's doing it to others as well.'

Charlie was pacing up and down the living room. 'What can be done? Where does she live, I want to go give her a piece of my mind.'

'I doubt she'll be there; she's already moved onto her next woman; she told me she had a date when I saw her last. It's awful to think she's going to do the same to someone else. I'm guessing there is nothing we can do?'

'Not really no, it's bloody awful though. There should be a website where you can report dodgy women. Mind you I'd have been on that list for a different reason in the past. What are you going to do now?'

'Don't be daft Charlie, there's a massive difference from you and Helen. She's a narcissist, you just didn't want to settle down until you found Alice.'

'Tactful,' laughed Charlie. 'So what are you going to do now, any ideas?'

'I was thinking on the way here, I might go join my parents for the Nile cruise, they will be pretty much done with the Orient Express and Venice by now, I'm sure I could sort something.'

'That sounds a brilliant idea. Is there anything you need us to do?'

'No it's ok, I'll just leave my keys with Lou and ask her to bring the post in, make sure the house is ok. I think a break will do me good, it's been a long time since I have properly just put everything down and relaxed. Maybe while I'm away I can think of where I go from here.'

'Very true. Remember we're always here if you need us. And maybe later in the year we'll be business partners? Ashfield Farm agreed on a price this afternoon. We're going to be farmers and wedding planners, how brilliant is that.'

'If anyone can do it it's you two. I just need to find someone to marry.'

'In time I'm sure you will, but for now just chill and try and forget what's happened, heal as the guru's say. You've got us all behind you,' said Alice.

'I know, I'm so grateful to you all. It could all have ended so differently.'

'But it didn't, you will be stronger because of it. Just you see. Now do you want a hand finding flights and stuff?' asked Charlie rubbing her hands together.

Grace smiled and nodded; she knew she'd come to the right place.

'Let's get you down the Nile, hopefully without any murders!'

Epilogue?

The walls of the York Union Workhouse loomed ahead as Eliza and Gertrude walked with their mothers through the snowstorm, towards the huge, black metal gates. It was the dead of winter, snow lay heavy upon the ground and their shoeless feet, frozen like blocks of ice, left small imprints on the path. Their mothers had tried their hardest after the death of their husbands to keep food on the table for the two girls, but life was cruel when you started off with nothing, and char work was hard to find.

The sorry group were met at the entrance by the Guardian, a large bulbous nosed man, who stood at the door wearing a thick brown woollen suit, large black coat and a well-worn cane. He showed no emotion on his ugly face as he let the four into the workhouse and directed them into a stark wood panelled room which had a roaring fire which the children were drawn to like magnets.

A woman came into the room, her pock marked face was illuminated by the light from the fire as she pulled the girls away and pushed them towards their mothers who were stood behind a desk where a leather-bound ledger was open on a partially blank page. He entered the date at the top of the fresh page 8th December 1850.

"Names" said the Guardian briskly as he scribbled down the names of the four Anne and Eliza Dagnell, and Ruth and Gertrude Marr spoken by their mothers. "How old are thee" he said looking at the girls.

"Both ten" said Anne Dagnell, her daughter hiding behind her.

"Cat got her tongue" asked the foul woman, warming her arse after hitching up her long dress.

"No, she's very tired, we've walked from Elvington in this weather," said Anne. "We're all tired."

"Pah, summat up with thee, nowt between their ears by looks of it," said the Guardian. "Take em up to the children's ward, I'll take these two t' women's. Say goodbye to your mothers" he said in the coldest voice any of them had ever heard, even that of the rent collector from their last tenement.

"Please, can't we stay together, we've never been apart" said Anne, holding onto her daughter as though her life depended on it, although she knew it was hopeless. Everyone knew that children were separated from their parents, women from their husbands, the elderly from the young, the lunatics from the sane. All in the hope of stopping the poor being reliant on the systems put in place to control them.

"Get thee gone woman, show some backbone" as he flapped his hands in the direction of the entrance to the workhouse. The two mothers hugged their girls tightly before being shooed along the corridor into the bowels of the building, the Guardian following close behind.

Gertrude and Eliza stood in the middle of the room, their hands clasped together as a form of comfort, fear in their eyes but neither of them shedding the tears that wanted to fall. Little did they know that was the final time they would ever see their mothers.

The pock faced woman let down her skirts and grabbed each girl by the top of her arm and headed them all in the same direction as their mothers had gone but they were nowhere to be seen, the sounds of doors and keys could be heard in the distance, along with the wailing of an unhappy baby. The girls were forced into a room where a large cast iron bath stood with grey scummed water.

"Get tha clothes off and put them ova there" she pointed in the direction of a wooden crate in the corner of the room. "And hurry up about it, I ain't got all day".

Gertrude and Eliza stripped off their damp clothes and put them in the box, then one by one they were directed onto a wooden chair where the woman took a large pair of scissors and cut off all their hair leaving only stubble on what had once been long dark locks.

"Ya gotta get rid of the bugs, you're riddled" she said, "Now get in tha tub".

The girls got into the scummed water together where they were given a bar of stinky soap and told to scrub until their skin was clean. Gertrude and Eliza didn't take their eyes off each other, finding strength in being together in this miserable place.

Once bathed and dried hurriedly by the woman they were each given the workhouse uniform of dark grey pinafore dress and white apron, course socks and shoes that were tattered, but to the girls they were heaven from having been barefoot in the snow.

In the distance a clock struck eleven and taking a lit candle the girls were guided along dark corridors, passed doors that had quiet sobbing behind them, then reaching a long dormitory with a fire at one end the girls were told to lay down on straw beds with a threadbare blanket. Having somewhere to lay down that was dry and warm was an improvement on the damp room they had shared with other families until being evicted that day.

Swearing that they wouldn't be able to sleep, the girls dropped off through sheer exhaustion as the workhouse fell silent in the hours before dawn.

It was still dark when the workhouse bell rang loudly in the large room at 6am. The girls sat up stiffly in bed looking around at the dark shapes of other girls all waking suddenly. A different woman who had been ringing the bell shouted

"Gerrup. Gerrup. Inta tha clobber" she shouted. She was wearing a long black dress with black buttons down the front, holding the brass bell in her right hand, her left hand pointing towards the door at the top of the room.

The girls lined up at the door and Gertrude and Eliza followed suit. They had no idea what was happening, but they didn't want to be caught out doing the wrong thing. They were all marched down the long corridor and turned into another very large room which had long tables and benches lined along the length. The tables next to theirs had young boys and beyond them men both young and old, all wearing the same tattered clothes with shaved heads.

Bread on big wooden boards was placed in front of them and a bowl of grey porridge that the spoon stood up in, but the girls were grateful to have something in their empty bellies and the room was warm from the number of people in them and the fires that were lit at each end. They were each given a mug of milk which was warm and had a skin on it, but they all slurped it happily, so relieved to have something inside them. The room was silent except for the scrapping of plates and the smacking of lips. Eliza looked around the room longing to see her mother, even just a glimpse to know that all was well, but she was too small to see beyond the tables of men who blocked the way. A small boy was crying silent tears into his food, he made brief eye contact with Gertrude but they both looked away for fear of joining in the sadness that enveloped the room. Once the food was cleared two elderly women collected the plates and the tables of girls were ushered along the corridor and into a school room. The room had wooden panelling and a lit coal fire at one end next to a desk where a strict looking woman with her hair scraped into a bun on the top of her head sat.

Neither of the girls had been to school, they had moved around too much for that and their parents couldn't read nor write so the mechanics of the day were totally alien to them. They were each given a piece of chalk and a slate and were told to follow the instructions on the large blackboard in the corner. The object of which was to form letters of the alphabet but neither girl understood why that was.

Lunch of bread and cheese was followed by religious instruction and hell and damnation preached if they wasted food or didn't follow the rules that were hung on the walls. Not that the girls could read them, so they both sat silent for fear of breaking one of these unknown rules.

Arithmetic followed this with strange numbers being written on the board and the girls again tried to follow how to write them out, being shouted at for getting the figures wrong and for looking so puzzled. The whole room of girls scratching marks on the black slate in the hope of approval.

Dinner followed, some sort of meat in a bowl with some vegetables and some bread and another mug of warm milk. Then once finished all the girls stood and filed back to the dormitory, Eliza and Gertrude tagged behind them, heads bowed with tiredness and sadness of being apart from their mothers.

It all seemed so regimented, the day broken up by school lessons, religious instruction and food, then bed. All accompanied by various stern women in black, bearing the big brass bell which they rang to wake them, make them move, start eating, stop eating, go to bed and be quiet. The days in the workhouse turned to weeks, then to months, Christmas day went passed without much recognition other than extra religious instruction, this time by a drunk vicar who had come in to cleanse their souls and demanding their repentance for sins yet to be committed. The two girls fell into the daily routine, keeping their heads down, trying to learn to write, managing to learn their names and to be able to make a decent mark at it on the slate. They asked the other girls where their mothers were often, and once dared to ask if they could see them to one of the stern black clad women, but each time they were told they were being kept apart for their own good.

However, one March morning instead of filing to the dining room, 8 of the girls were separated from the others and taken to the Guardians office. No explanation was given, just told to follow a woman with the brass bell. Once in the office the bulbous nosed Guardian was sat at the desk with another man stood in front of the fire warming his hands.

"These are the lasses I told you about, the lads have been chosen and will be along in a minute. Can you sign these documents to keep things square?" he said

The man that was stood by the fire went to the desk and took the pen and signed his name at the bottom.

The door opened and 8 boys came into the room, they were all shaven headed and had stiff jaws trying hard to look confident at this unfolding situation. They stood in the corner of the room looking at their feet, hands in their pockets.

"Stand up straight lads, straight backs, show the man you are fit for work," said the Guardian.

The boys and girls all looked at each other.

"Line up across there," he said pointing to the wall near the entrance to the workhouse.

The children all lined up as instructed, Gertrude and Eliza locked fingers behind their backs to try and stop their hands from shaking, they didn't understand what was happening and they were as terrified as the other children and were trying hard to not show it.

The man walked up to each of them and looked them up and down.

"They're a bit on the scrawny side but will have to do, I'll take em. Right you lot, you're coming to work at the mill at Fewston, fresh air will do you good, soon put some meat on tha bones" he said getting out a pocket watch. "Better get a move on to get there before dark, me wagons outside".

There were audible gasps and frantic looks on the children's faces. Gertrude squeezed Eliza's hand hard making her let out a small yelp, but no one noticed, they were all in their own private hell.

The Guardian opened the door, and the man shook his hand. "Right out you go, you could look a bit grateful" he said sneering at the children. The Guardian laughed.

The boys went first, their eyes fearful and one of the girls began to cry for her mother. It was then that it struck them all that they would not see their parents again. Feet dragged to the wagon and horses tethered at the side of the road outside. It was drizzling and the wooden sided wagon offered little protection to the elements. Most of the children climbed into the wagon but one small boy refused and was picked up and thrown into the container, letting out a scream as he fell against some metal tools hidden in the straw on the floor. His leg began to bleed, and he whimpered in both fear and pain. Gertrude and Eliza, afraid of making a scene, feeling torn between running away and obeying, trudged towards the wagon where their legs climbed up to join the others, sitting down on the straw with the other children. There was a pile of blankets in the corner and one of the older boys passed them around to all the children who huddled together for warmth.

The mill man climbed up behind the horses taking the reins and geeing up the horses to a steady trot, the workhouse disappearing into the distance as they headed towards York centre. The horse's hooves were but a dull thud on the sand road, which changed to an echoing clip clop as the horses went through Monk Bar onto Goodramgate, close to where Gertrude and Eliza had once lived in a slum behind the main street. The wagon carried on down Church Street, passed the market and over Ouse Bridge, then they were rattled as the wheels went over the cobbles of Micklegate under the barbican and out onto Tadcaster Road which was the furthest that either of the girls had ever travelled before, but never on a wagon. The city disappeared behind them as they turned and went down narrow roads before finally entering the greenery of the countryside.

The rain stopped and the sun began to shine through the grey clouds, passing hedgerows with cows and sheep huddled in gateways. The girls had seen farm animals before at the cattle market at the Barbican, but never in fields, and had never seen the stunning views of the hills in the distance, nor farmhouses with rows of neat washing hanging on lines. Their mothers had taken in washing to earn money but theirs was never so bright, nor as fresh looking.

The injured boy looked stricken, the blood had stopped flowing from his leg, but he looked pale and shaky, the congealed blood drying on the straw around him. The children all travelled in silence, full of fear and sadness at what lay ahead for them and for the family they had left behind.

The wagon journeyed on, the swaying and creaking of the boards eventually sent some of the children to sleep like some weird lullaby, the wood rhythmically groaning out a beat on the uneven road. The sun continued to shine and the straw around them warmed them along with the blankets which kept out some of the cold.

The wagon turned off the road and into a forested area, the track became very bumpy, and the horse slowed down to a walk, the trees at times blocking out most of the light as they arched over the lane. Hedging was replaced by dry stone walls with rolling hills and stone cottages and barns dotted around the landscape. They felt far removed from York and the built up, dirty streets. The wagon turned up a wider lane and into a village with stone cottages lining the street, with smoke coming out of chimneys and a church in the centre. In the graveyard a vicar stood over an open grave, the words of prayer drifting towards the wagon which came to a stop. The vicar closed his bible and came down the lane, opening a wooden gate and approached the mill man.

"Morning Vicar is that one of ours?" asked the mill man.

The children could see the vicar stood through the slats in the wagon, he looked sad and tired.

"Yes Jack, it's one of your lasses. Who's in the back?" he asked sternly looking towards the back of the wagon.

"A few waifs and strays from the workhouse, got to keep the workforce up vicar, business is business" he said laughing. "Better life for them up here than in there".

"Is it? Is it really Jack. There's too many of your workers in my graveyard, how can that be right?" the vicar asked.

"Just bad luck, weak parents make weak kids" Jack replied.

"No!" shouted the vicar. "Poverty and greed make weak children. You should be ashamed of yourself and those like you".

"Pah, if their parents hadn't been so lazy then their kids wouldn't be here would they, I'm doing society a favour taking them off the hands of the workhouse" said Jack gathering up the reins. "Bye vicar".

And with that he geed up the horses who broke into a trot and they sped out of the village up into the hills. A short while later the horses slowed down as they turned into a cobbled road and then came to a halt. Jack jumped down and came round the back of the wagon, letting down the back ramp.

"Out ya get" he bellowed.

All the children obeyed, clambering down from the wagon onto the cobbles. In front of them was a beautiful vista of trees, hills and luscious greenery, however they were turned away from it and guided towards a large stone building, each window was small and had bars on the outside, the entrance door was metal and solid. Jack was joined by an old woman, and an older boy and girl who ushered the children inside. The child with the injured leg limping at the back, trying hard to keep up was pushed along by the older boy. They were shoved and separated into lines of boys and girls then led off in separate directions. The building was cold, damp and silent, so Gertrude and Eliza were surprised when a door opened and there were many other girls of various ages sat on beds in the room.

"Get yourself a bed and settle down. If you're quiet, we'll bring you some food," said the old woman.

The girls doubled up into the spare single beds, each of which had two blankets folded on them. Gertrude and Eliza took the bed by a window, the draft could be felt as they sat there in silence, too afraid to speak or move from where they had been told to go. They pulled the blankets around them, cuddling up for warmth and comfort.

Shortly after the older girl appeared with a large jug of milk, a loaf of bread and block of cheese on a tray, which she put on a table in the far corner the room.

"Come get some grub, new lasses first, you look famished" she said pouring the water into tin mugs.

Eliza took a piece of bread and a mug and handed them to Gertrude. "Where are we?" she asked the girl.

"Langdale Mill, where have you come from?" she asked.

"York, we're all from the workhouse. Why are we here?" asked Eliza.

"You're all here to work in the mill. I'm from Cheapside in London and have been here years. I'm Clara," she said continuing to distribute mugs and slabs of bread to the other children.

"Years?" cried Gertrude, "What about our mams? Will they come here too?"

Clara tilted her head with a sympathetic look on her face. "No, none of us have seen our parents in a long time, my mam was taken to an asylum and I went into the workhouse and not been able to find out what happened to her then".

Gertrude began to silently sob, big fat tears rolling down her cheeks, turning her face to the wall so no one could see her. Eliza held her hand, feeling equally bereft but didn't want to show the room how scared she was.

"Eat up and get some sleep. It's an early start tomorrow. I'm in the bed near the door" she said getting up and taking off her outer clothes and getting into bed wearing her under slip. Gertrude and Eliza followed suit, climbing into their bed together, hugging each other for warmth and comfort.

To be continued

Thank you for buying and reading my second novel, I hope that you have enjoyed reading it as much as I did writing it.

I will be eternally grateful if you would put a review on Amazon, especially a written one. Writers love to know what journey the story has taken you down, what parts you loved, the characters that you want to be your best friends.

Again thank you for reading and I will crack on with book 3. Where will Charlie and Alice go next?

Printed in the USA
CPSIA information can be obtained
at www.ICGtesting.com
LVHW050904271124
797754LV00002B/109